NAVIGATE

NAVIGATE

HOW THE BIBLE CAN HELP YOU
IN EVERY ASPECT OF YOUR LIFE

NORMAN VINCENT PEALE

New York

Navigate

ISBN-10: 0-8249-3219-6
ISBN-13: 978-0-8249-3219-0

Published by Guideposts
16 East 34th Street
New York, New York 10016
Guideposts.org

Distributed by Ideals Publications, a Guideposts company
2630 Elm Hill Pike, Suite 100
Nashville, Tennessee 37214

Guideposts and *Ideals* are registered trademarks of Guideposts.

Acknowledgments

Every attempt has been made to credit the sources of copyrighted material used in this book. If any such acknowledgment has been inadvertently omitted or miscredited, receipt of such information would be appreciated.

All Scripture quotations are taken from *The Holy Bible, New International Version*. Copyright © 1973, 1978, 1984, 2011 by Biblica, Inc. Used by permission of Zondervan. All rights reserved worldwide. www.zondervan.com

Library of Congress Cataloging-in-Publication Data has been applied for.

Cover and interior design by Müllerhaus
Cover image of ship engraving by Gustave Doré
Cover image of compass by Shutterstock
Author photograph courtesy of the Peale family
Typeset by Aptara, Inc.

Printed and bound in the United States of America
10 9 8 7 6 5 4 3 2 1

CONTENTS

CONTENTS

FOREWORD

Thank you for your interest in the work of Norman Vincent Peale. We hope you'll find his words as deeply rewarding and potentially life-changing as we did. Each entry will be framed around one or more relevant Scripture verses, and discuss several conflicts, issues, occurrences, etc., that we face in the occasionally troubling world we live in. And each difficulty is responded to using carefully selected thoughts and anecdotes on the meaning and applicability of Scripture in daily life and the practical advice garnered from Dr. Peale's long life spent serving God and preaching His Word. The syntax has been slightly modified for our time but has preserved the true timelessness of Dr. Peale's original message of hope, toughness, and love, as well as his enduringly warm wit, knowledge and affectionate presence.

—The Editors of Guideposts

NAVIGATE

INTRODUCTION

Do you really know how to deal successfully with difficulties? Do you handle things with a sense of control, knowing that you can cope with the changing circumstances of everyday existence? Or do you tend to fall apart, and become depressed and hopeless about your situation? These are important questions for us all.

For anyone whose life is confused, disorganized, frustrated or lacking in energy and strength, the best thing to do is to get healed of such negatives and become filled with faith. You might say, "But you don't know how tough my life is. I have real problems!"

I am not unaware of how much heartache and struggle there is in human existence. How could I be? I've spent countless afternoons reading the hundreds and hundreds of letters from broken families struggling with abuse, runaway children, drugs, disease, sin, alcoholism, failure, unemployment, loneliness, bereavement. If these letters were put together and published in a book, it would be a total history of human sadness and misery: the gamut of human problems. And yet, we all know of people who, despite their difficulties, manage to pull together and make something profound or powerful happen, through their sheer force of will. I think, more than not, that sheer force of will I referred to stems from a potent, solid faith that drives a man or woman to excel at the highest level. God made us in His image, and we can do right by Him by intending to live in a Godly way.

Moreover, the Bible can help you. That is what this book is about. Its aim is the definite, practical purpose that can be found in a mature understanding of how the Bible gives real help for real problems.

The Bible is a book of faith. As such, it is the history of God's dealing with men and women. It contains the greatest of all philosophy. It outlines the plan of salvation. It explains the origin and purpose of the world. It deals with man and woman and their relation to God. It shows God as the Creator, the Alpha, the Omega. These are all very great and important matters. But the Bible is so much more than a history of man. It is also a deeply rich compendium of God's wisdom, His help and His desire to see to it that *all* of His children lead a life filled with faith and love in their hearts— not lost, confused, numb or stumbling in the darkness, but found, saved, comforted by grace. And yet, many people do not know how to let the Bible help them.

The purpose of this book, then, and the purpose of the Bible are one and the same: to save you when you need help the most and to help supplement your knowledge of the Word even when you're fortunate enough to not need any help! The wise man, knowing that difficulty is a part of life, will look for ways to become strong in advance, gaining strength that comes through knowing Him. Or, as Psalm 46:10 teaches us, "Be still, and know that I am God."

My purpose is merely to open a few more doors by which you may pass into the riches of the Scriptures. As a result of this book and your trusty Bible—the best of all books, indeed this greatest library of all books, will, in time, open up Truth for you in such a way that will change your life in a manner that is wonderful indeed.

You do not need to struggle with defeat, nor live in sorrow. You do not need to give in to weakness and sin, nor hold hate in your heart. Let the Bible help you. It really can, and more effectively than you may imagine. By dwelling on Scripture—and more importantly, ultimately living by them, with them, in togetherness with God—you make ready for whatever challenge comes, when and if it comes. God bless.

DESPAIR VS. GRACE

"Then Jesus beholding him loved him, and said unto him,
One thing thou lackest: go thy way, sell whatsoever thou
hast, and give to the poor, and thou shalt have treasure
in heaven: and come, take up the cross, and follow me."

–Mark 10:21

How can one become what assuredly God meant him to be, namely, a graceful person, for lack of a better word? This question was suggested by a young man who came for a chat. He opened by asking directly "Why don't people like me?"

He was about thirty-five and well-groomed, rather exceptionally so in fact. He proceeded to outline certain circumstances and incidents in which he had run afoul of human relations. "I do my best," he explained. "I try to put into practice all the rules I've been taught about getting along with people. I have really worked at it." (Obviously he was sincere.) "But I do not succeed."

There was in his manner of speech a veiled criticism, thinly veiled but nonetheless apparent. His lips pursed in such a way as to indicate a kind of reproof for everybody, as if he had just a bit of disdain for other people. There was about him a marked superiority and rigidity, a primness.

Then he asked, "Please tell me, is there some workable procedure by which I can become an attractive person and have people like me?" The more I meditated upon his question, the more the realization grew that this is a problem faced by many. It is not a light or flippant theme, it is a problem of first-rate importance.

The head of personnel of a large corporation told me that over a period of years he had learned that most people fail not because of a lack of ability or training or unwillingness to learn and progress, but basically because of an inability to adjust satisfactorily to other people. Some quality in our nature, some friction in personality, throws up a real and substantial barrier through which we cannot pass to establish that easy rapport by which we attain smooth relationships with other human beings. People whose faces would be lovely do not realize the enormous value of a pleasant look. A thin, filmy unpleasantness gets over their faces and makes them forbidding.

Speaking of a rather brilliant woman whose achievements were outstanding, another woman said to me, "What a marvel she would be if she could only get a radiance." In other words she had everything but that last something called radiance. I cannot help but remember the sunlight that streams through my church some mornings. Doesn't it make a difference? As compared to a rainy day? All that it is, is a path of sunlight; yet it is a radiance, it is the extra glory, it is the added beauty that makes a great difference in the atmosphere.

Now how do you get this thing, this attractiveness that makes a personality lovable? A remarkable picture of a human being was read to us in the Scripture passage, "And Jesus beholding him, loved him." We say that occasionally about people: "great fellow," "charming lady," "salt of the earth," "great soul." Looking upon a person we love them, everybody loves them, they exude a native-born attractiveness. Analyze that and you will find it always flows from some simple thing. For one thing they are not sharp. Some people are sharp, as if they have points sticking out all over them. They ought to be called human porcupines. Some people are easy to get along with; they are like an old shoe or an old hat—they fit you comfortably. It is a great art to be that way.

It is a pathetic thing when you are somebody who has to be handled with care. People have to watch out for you. They say, "Be careful of him or you are likely to get into trouble." Now that kind of person is not what you would call one who has attained lovability or attractiveness. But you object, "I am what I am, this is the way I was born." I must take exception. It is not the way you were born. You were never determined to be what you are. You made yourself that way. There is no study of heredity today by which you can rationalize your unattractiveness, none at all. You can do anything with yourself. Any human being can make himself by the grace of God as he wants to be. You were not born that way. You developed that way. I am not going to blame my mother and father for what I am now. What I am now I made myself. So help me God.

But there is a way in which you can remake yourself. There is a marvelous way in which any human being in this world can be refashioned so that he can walk the earth with amazing attractiveness, getting the homage of his fellow men. Henry Drummond who wrote a book called *Love, the Greatest Thing in the World*, which incidentally is one of the greatest books ever written in the history of the English language, tells us that "it is the most astounding thing what happened to a tax gatherer and a fisherman and a farmer and small business men (the disciples) when they lived with Jesus." They were average men. They had all the faults and failings of human nature. Often they were an irrational, antagonistic lot. But as Henry Drummond reminded us, "as they lived with Jesus over the months, they changed as the marvelous alchemy of His spirit had His way with them." They became immortal figures for all time, these simple fishermen, a tax gatherer and others.

On one occasion two of these men, Peter and John, were hailed before the leaders of the state and they spoke with such persuasive power, they conducted themselves with such decorum, they revealed such personal qualifications and gifts that those who watched were astounded. They had initially perceived Peter and John to be ignorant and unlearned men, but were instead filled with astonishment. They could not believe they were the same men. They exclaimed that one is just a fisherman and just an ordinary fellow. He used to get mad at everybody, had a high temper. The other has always been considered unstable.

Then the Bible explains, "When they saw Peter and John and perceived that they were ignorant and unlearned, they took knowledge of them." That is to say, they figured it out. They took knowledge of them that they had been with Jesus. They had come under his influence. He had laid His hand upon them. He breathed his spirit into them and they had become different. They became rare and attractive persons.

What had happened to them? It's really quite remarkable, isn't it? But the most remarkable thing, I'll tell you, is that this can happen to us also! He filled their hearts with love. He can happily do the same thing for you. It is only sensible to approach people in a kindly manner. They then returned the kindliness. Live in a spirit of love, like Jesus, and you have what is necessary to make people like you. Practice love and after awhile you become lovable. It is said if you cast your bread on the waters it comes back to you after many days. If a person practices love in his relationships to other people, love comes back to him as certain as there is a law that lifts the tide. It is love that makes us attractive.

I was on an overnight flight not long ago and when I got on the plane the very amiable flight attendant greeted me, "Glad to see you. How are you today?"

"Well," I said, "I am all right." I was astonished at his reception. I got into my seat and another attendant happened by, beamed, and said, "Hello there. How are you? How are you feeling today?"

"Well," I said, somewhat amusedly. "I am all right."

I was amazed at this astounding concern for my physical well-being. I had always been treated well by airline employees but today there was an extra something in the air. Then I remembered the advertisements I had read of this particular airline. Sometimes I think advertisements are a little tricky, or insincere, but nevertheless this airline apparently instructed their people to fall back on that great thing that used to characterize American business: service with a smile. These people were not only putting a smile on but a laugh as well. It was full-on kindliness. I settled into my seat and was working on some manuscripts. Two women were sitting across the aisle from me who were rather along in years and one of them was doing an enormous job of complaining. She was complaining about her husband, she was complaining about her children, she was complaining about the house she lived in—she was just unhappy. You could see it written all over her. It must have been around ten o'clock in the evening when the flight attendant was making the rounds with drinks and snacks and said, "How are you this fine evening?" "Oh," she replied glumly, "I do not feel good."

Then I heard a wonderful thing. He said to her, "Well, I've got a pillow and a blanket right here with your name on them. Go to sleep. Get a good comfortable sleep so you can get up early and look down at the ocean. It's mighty pretty when the sun is shining on it."

The ocean is might pretty with the sun shining on it. Something about this young man's words touched a deep part of me. It resonated, his attitude of grace. I could see what it did to the woman across the aisle. She smiled sheepishly and was sound asleep in no more than twenty minutes. I soon became aware that this flight attendant was one of the most well-loved individuals on our flight because his heart was bubbling over with love for people. He talked to this woman, twenty years older than himself, like a father who would say to his little girl, "You are sleepy and tired; that is why you are so irritable, go to bed. Get a good sleep." I did not inquire into the life of this flight attendant for I could see it in his face. Somewhere along the line as he made his trips he had undoubtedly been with Jesus.

That is the way to be a graceful human being: get all hate, ill will, self-pity and self-consciousness out of your heart. Get away from domination by yourself through loving people. That is the way to do it. When you go home to dinner, practice with your family. That is the best place to start. Sit across the table and just start loving your spouse. Did you ever stop to think of the marvelous wisdom and power of Jesus? He simply said, "Love one another."

But that is not the whole matter. There is another quality, which is hard to describe. How can you describe love? How can you describe sunlight? How can you describe something that you cannot hold in your hand? That you cannot diagram? Well I have seen and you have seen persons who have a, shall we call it, a dynamic quality, a vibration, an alertness, a marvelous beauty, an infectious quality, so that you were literally spellbound by them, so that you were caught by them, so that you exclaim, "What is there about this person that grips me so? Is it intellectual power? Is it fame or honor? Or is it some magnetism within touched by something from without?"

Now the great thing about Jesus Christ is that when He really touches a personality He performs a curious transformation. Perhaps I can best describe it by this illustration. I do not want you to get the idea I travel all the time, but this trip that I described a moment ago finally took me to Richmond, Virginia, where I addressed a large mass meeting. A minister took me for a ride around Richmond and showed me the historical places. He is a great fellow with a typical, delightful, southern accent, and he is a marvelous storyteller.

He said, "This Gospel that you and I preach is more wonderful than we realize. The trouble with us is we do not make it simple enough. We think when we preach a sermon we have to be profound. Maybe if we just told the simple story of Jesus Christ and let it stand that would be enough. Some time ago," he continued, "a group of students from a theological seminary asked me to give them a talk on 'What is Christianity,' at a local meeting in one of the churches in the city and all young persons were invited to come. Those students, those young scholars, had their notebooks ready to write down my 'profound' definition of Christianity. Suddenly it came over me that I would just tell them a simple, simple story. So I told them as simply as I could just what Christianity is. Then I opened the meeting to discussion and asked if there were anybody there who would like to give his definition of Christianity. One by one the students spoke—and when you are studying in a theological school you are wiser than you will ever be thereafter.

"Finally a young girl about twenty or twenty-one arose and in a charming manner said, 'Mr. Chairman, I am a stranger in town. Would it be all right for me to speak?' She was not what you would call pretty in a sophisticated sense of the word, indeed she was rather an ordinary, plain girl. She said, 'I would like to give a definition if you don't mind. Once there was a man, a wonderful man and His name was Jesus Christ and He was born long ago into the home of a carpenter. He went out under the stars and walked the roadways and sat on the hillside and men gathered around Him and He talked with them, and He had a wonderful way about Him. Bad men plotted against Him and one day they hung Him on a cross and killed Him and when He died everybody was sad. That was not the end. If that had been the end of it there would be nothing to talk about. But He rose again and He lives and wherever a human being turns to Him they find Him and He helps them. He helps them with all their problems and their difficulties and He makes life so wonderful for all of us.'"

This minister said that as he watched her, this plain girl was transformed into a most beautiful woman. A light flooded her countenance and flashed from her eyes and her hair seemed to become soft and lustrous. He shook his head with wonder. "In that moment, to all of us, she was inexpressibly beautiful."

When Jesus has truly looked upon us, and we've taken in His message, His Word and accepted His love—and we treat other people with that knowledge, that reverence and that love in the forefront of our personhood—we become immensely loveable, much in the way that Jesus loved: we become graceful. We radiate love.

ON UNHAPPINESS

Many people are vaguely unhappy. But really they don't need to be. One can awaken every morning with a thrill, looking forward with anticipation to the day. You can image having the time of your life all day long and actually regret having to go to bed for fear of missing something exciting.

Three verses will help you cast off unhappiness and show you how to live joyously. We suggest that you say the first one out loud every day: "This is the day which the Lord hath made; let us rejoice and be glad in it" (Psalm 118:24).

Those words are a stimulating mental and spiritual tonic with which to begin the day. Upon awakening, say these dynamic words out loud. You have a new day crammed with opportunity to build a better and happier life. As you go to work, repeat the verse and, if you begin to run down in spirit during the day, say it again. This is one of the greatest of all strength producing thoughts. Possibly no method is more effective for driving off unhappiness than to saturate the mind with these powerful words.

"Rejoice in the Lord always again I will say, Rejoice" (Philippians 4:4). You can make yourself unhappy by habitually thinking unhappy thoughts. Instead start thinking joyfully. It is that simple. Practice rejoicing, not vaguely, but specifically rejoicing in the Lord. Think of every wonderful thing the Lord has done for you, the most important being that He is always with you. When you consider the implications of that fact, there is every reason to rejoice and be happy, for it means that nothing can ever defeat you.

"These things I have spoken to you...that your joy might be full" (John 15:11). Real, in-depth Christians are always happy people. Of course, that does not mean that they are free from pain and suffering, but they have the power to conquer it. They are filled with joyous exultation, for they have the priceless experience of victory over misery. To be happy, try to follow the "things" Jesus teaches. You will experience joy in its fullest form.

DO NOT STUMBLE

Behold, I give unto you power to tread on serpents
and scorpions, and over all the power of the
enemy: and nothing shall by any means hurt you.

–Luke 10:19

Many people today are stumbling through life half-defeated. A distinguished literary person showed me a recent report by the American Library Association indicating the type of books that are most requested today. The demand for books dealing with domestic and international affairs has declined. Fiction is declining. Romance novels are declining. The great demand in the libraries and bookstores today is for books that tell people how to solve their problems, how to get some personal power.

Standing in front of a large congregation, as I do several times a week, is a very interesting way to study faces. Naturally I know many faces in my own congregation, many I do not. Yet anybody who knows anything about human nature realizes that in so large a congregation as mine there are many who, while appearing outwardly self-contained and in full possession of themselves, nevertheless are defeated. They are haunted by fears, they are abnormally sensitive to criticism, they are easily hurt, they give the impression outwardly of being dominating, but inwardly they are shrinking, with a profound sense of inadequacy and inferiority. They awaken in the night with anxiety and apprehension about the future. They are in conflict within themselves and sometimes in conflict outside of themselves. There is no peace or composure in them, no masterful grip upon themselves. They are governed by whims and fancies. They are victims of their own lack of control.

That is a sad and sorry picture of a person who is stumbling through life half-defeated. There is no power in such a personality because I have just mentioned a few points at which power leaks away. On the other hand, in my congregation, there are very fortunate people who have had an experience of God whereby the peace and power of God has come into their minds and hearts. They have learned to be masters of their worries and their fears. They are organized and integrated personalities. They are not divided. They are not in conflict either with themselves or with others. They have become masters of the technique of living. All their powers are functioning, they are not stumbling through life, they are reaching and bounding through life with energy and with joy. They are in possession of power—a gift from God.

The great thing is that everybody here today can have this power. It is promised to you, it is offered you; all you have to do is take it. Look back at the Scripture quote that opens this chapter. Read it, out loud if you can, several times. Of course, it is stated in the picturesque imagery of the Bible...power over serpents, slimy, sinister things that slither through your life, awful terrors, dark and malevolent things—that is marvelous. And scorpions, even more venomous and deadly. Does that not describe many a person's condition at his worst moments? Serpents and scorpions of fear and hate and of nervous tension, irritability, sin—all the enemies—behold, He says, "Behold, I give unto you power to tread on serpents and scorpions, and over all the power of the enemy: and nothing shall by any means hurt you."

Now, that does not mean you will not receive some injury in your life. It does not mean you will not get old. It does not mean great disappointments will not come to you, but it does mean that with this kind of power nothing shall ever hurt you to ruin you. No disappointment, no frustrations, no opposition can ever really hurt you. You cast it off as though you were clad in armor, indeed you are, not armor of steel but armor of the Spirit. It will not destroy you nor discourage you, nor frustrate you, nothing shall ever hurt the real you or dethrone you from the mastery of your life.

I believe in this with all my heart. I wish that I might be given just one glorious moment to drive it into your mind so you will accept it and never forget it, that you by the grace of God do not need to be defeated by anything in this world, that you can have power to meet any circumstance or any situation. Moreover you can get it right here today and believe me you had better get it because the assaults of life upon us are tremendous.

"I have given you authority." Now how does He give it to us? Not in any mysterious way. There is nothing mysterious in the mechanism of Christianity. It is a scientific thing based on law—the law of God. Do you mean to tell me that the same God who puts into the world the laws that lift the tides, the law that governs the succession of the seasons, the God Who puts into the world the laws of machinery and electricity, does not operate according to law in the matters of the spiritual world? In my humble opinion the New Testament is a Book of law, wonderful statements of scientific law through which if you will learn and practice them you will get a definite result.

All power is channeled to us through mechanisms. We have power on Sunday in church. We have power when we're sitting in a folding chair in the waiting room at our dentist's office. There is electric light—that is power, it comes from a certain mechanism. The heat to warm our homes comes through mechanisms, coils, wires and vents. Spiritual power is also received through mechanisms. You can take a human being no matter how defeated he is and study him and analyze him, and then apply to him spiritual mechanisms and he can get definite results in power. I have seen it happen many times.

Not long ago, for example, a man came to see me, one of the most defeated personalities I think I have ever seen. This man, thirty-eight years of age, came literally crawling into my office. He was hunched over and painfully slunk into a seat. I said, "How old did you say you were?"

He said, "Thirty-eight." (I could easily have believed he was seventy-eight from his attitude.) "I am an awful sick man." (I thought he was sick, too, but he was not sick in the way he thought he was.) "A few months ago," he explained, "I had a terrible attack one night and they had to take me to a hospital and put me under an oxygen tent. I thought it was a heart attack, but it was not. My heart has reacted all right; the doctor told me there was nothing wrong with my heart, nothing wrong with my blood pressure. I went to the mental ward—where they put me through all the tests and there is nothing wrong with me physically. I went to one of the greatest doctors in my section of the country and he cannot find anything wrong. They all sent me to a psychiatrist. The psychiatrist says that all I have to do is practice a little faith. That is how I happened to get around to see you."

I began to pry around at him, found that he had lived a very decent, upright life. That was his reputation. That was his honest statement to me—it was not made out of guilt. But I found the trouble in this young man's relationship with his father. His father was a large man and apparently quite dominating. His father took his son as a very young boy into the store and put him to work after school and all vacations, never allowing him to play baseball or other sports after school and Saturdays. His father told him exactly what he should do. He was not the same kind of man his father was, either in size or in strength or in mental slant. Then one or two tragedies happened in the family, all of them connected with mental troubles and he became afraid he was going to have the same experience. He never married for fear his children would have the disease. His whole life was riddled with fear, plus resentment. I gave him the opportunity for the first time in his life to express the resentment he had developed against his father. He did it with hesitancy and with agony for he respected and loved his father, yet this resentment was there. I told him it was not being disloyal to his father to get cured of his illness.

Then I told him how a physician in this city answered my question as to what caused most disease among his patients: "Seventy-five per cent of the people who come to me are basically ill because of either fear or resentment or both."

"Can a person have the real attributes of illness through fear and resentment?" I asked. He said, "He can, I believe, die from fear and resentment."

The sickly man who'd come to see me realized that he was that kind of case. He asked me, "Can I ever have power?" I said, "Yes, you can." There was a time in my ministry when I would have merely prayed with him and told him to put his faith in God, which is what I did tell him but put in a different way. I wrote him out a prescription. I did not put the "Rx" up at the top because I am not legally empowered to do that, but it is a prescription, nonetheless. This was the prescription. "Several times each day, preferably out loud, make the following statements: (1) Through God's goodness nothing is wrong with me save my wrong thinking which is now being corrected. This is happening at this moment, not in the future. It is happening now. (2) I believe in the possibility of a happy, effective life. (3) God is now filling my mind, my body and my soul with peace, courage and strength. (4) I completely surrender myself to God and trust Him for the saving of my life. I put myself completely in His hands. God is giving me strength to do my work each day and He is preparing for me a happy and useful future; therefore, I will have no fear, I will be filled with love, I will go ahead with confidence."

I said, "Take that home and say all of that a half dozen times a day. Practice believing them and I believe in time your mental attitudes will change. This process can change your life for the better."

For twenty-five years he had been thinking in terms of fear and resentment, and though you cannot change the fear thoughts and the resentment thoughts of twenty-five years in a moment, such thinking and reacting can be changed over a period of time. One who practices this truth will know the meaning of the words when He says, "I have given you authority to trample on snakes and scorpions and to overcome all the power of the enemy; nothing will harm you." This thing will work if you believe in these simple procedures and put them to work. Of course this procedure may sound a little new and different to you, but it is not so. It has been in the New Testament since it was written.

In the last analysis, the thing that brings power into human lives is something the preachers have been talking about since the beginning of Christian history, namely, conversion. It means that an individual becomes aware of his mistakes, his weakness, his defeat, realizing that he has no power of his own to change himself and so yields himself wholeheartedly and completely to Jesus Christ.

We are supposed to be a very enlightened people, but let me tell you that we will never get beyond the great fact that there is only one power that can change human nature, only one, and that is the power given to us by faith in Jesus Christ. If you are defeated by anything, if you will put this book down say out loud, "With all my heart I give myself to Thee," the great thing will happen to you. It happens to people every day. It is wonderful what great things happen to people who practice such faith in Christ.

I am going to share with you a letter. It is a letter written to me by a man who lives a long, long way from here. The writer is a businessman. Here is the letter:

"Dear Sir, For the past ten years I have been an increasingly heavy whiskey drinker. My age is now forty-seven. In the past few months I have gotten to the point of starting with a few drinks along from noon until bedtime and then usually waking up the next morning without being able to remember going to bed. Then too I was at the point where I could not shave and eat breakfast without one or two drinks to steady my nerves.

"In the past two months my problems have been fast multiplying in business and I was losing out on deal after deal, due to dreary thinking. Someone gave me a magazine which has a condensation of your new book, 'A Guide to Confident Living.' I scanned the first line and could not stop. I read it many times and I have taken your article out of the magazine and bound it. The formulas which you have put there I have memorized and I repeat them to myself while shaving in the morning. I was raised in a Christian home and was duly exposed to Sunday School and church as I grew up, but now for the first time in my life I am beginning to understand what faith, confidence and belief in a supreme God really mean in spiritual and practical sense.

"I am practicing mental control. When I have a flash thought of the unpleasant past I cut it off deliberately and by concentrating on the business problems of today I can feel the increased ability to forget the past. On getting out of bed and back to work I was able to close a deal in three days that I have fumbled for weeks. I have not had a drink of anything alcoholic since I read your condensed article. I have gained fifteen pounds and look five years younger. I go to bed before ten each night and arise with a song in my heart at daylight and read portions of your article and a few passages of the Bible and I think I am beginning to understand. I am doing this before the rest of the family are awake for they probably would not understand this complete about face. They are, of course, pleasantly aware that Daddy has not been drunk lately and the home life is somehow more agreeable. I have rediscovered the pleasure of helping our youngest, ten years old, with his homework in the evening and counseling with the twin boys, who are fifteen years old.

"You might like to know that I have been taking the boys to church and Sunday School each Sunday since I began this rehabilitation program. The fact is that last Sunday I joined the church where my wife has been a member for five years. Now get this—we have been married twenty-five years and I have not been a model husband by any means. I just muddled along being barely a husband and father and at times a drunken, sorry, vindictive, self-pitying creature. She had more courage to put up with me than I could ever muster. She joined the church, worked at it, read her Bible and prayed and worked hard each day for the family and for me.

"However, I had a glorious reward a few moments ago. I woke about midnight to feel a hand patting my cheek and tears dropping on my face and she was sitting there telling me how wonderful it was to have me sober and my old self again. I said to her, 'Why cry about it?' She replied, 'I cannot help it, I have prayed for it so long. While I was standing here by your bed and looking down at you I was overjoyed to see how pretty you were.' (I have always had a stern leathery face.) 'I was overjoyed to see how pretty you looked, sleeping so sound and peaceful, just like a little boy.' Then she added, 'I have always loved you but now it is such a joy to tell you how much I love you.' Suddenly all my hate, shame, rotten ideas and defeats of the past seemed to shed away like crumbling ashes of a burnt piece of paper and my love for her knew no bounds as I began to fully comprehend what she suffered all the time. So now, doctor, everybody and everything looks brighter to me since this happened." So concludes this letter.

See what happened? A man defeated, hopelessly defeated; all he does is read a magazine article, but the magazine article tells him to turn to Jesus Christ and the magazine article tells him how to turn to Jesus Christ and he does it and the change is so wonderful that he pours out his soul on paper, to tell about it. Many things change in this changing life of ours, but one thing never changes, and that is that amid the multitudes of New York City Christ still moves, the only One who can release men from themselves, the only One who can overcome their defeats, the only One who can give them victory.

He is still here and He says to you whatever your defeat may be: "I have given you authority to trample on snakes and scorpions and to overcome all the power of the enemy; nothing will harm you." Don't stumble through life half defeated, there's so much to overcome, and so much joy in doing so.

ON ANXIETY

Of all the thousands of letters I have received, the problem of worry is most frequently presented. The following verses helped many to gain victory over worries. Hence we can confidently say, The Lord is my helper I will not be afraid; what can man do to me? (Hebrews 13:6).

Nobody can really hurt you. We do not stand alone in this world for we can turn to God and He will always help us. Fill your mind with thoughts of God; get in harmony with God's will; eliminate from your mind all feelings contrary to love; practice simple trust. God then can help you. Practice thinking less about your worries and more about God. Instead of thinking how difficult your problem is, think how great and powerful God is. This will change your psychology; but more than that it releases spiritual power into your mind. That will enable you to meet your situation intelligently and creatively. Always repeat this text when you are afraid.

"Have no anxiety about anything, but in everything by prayer and supplication with thanksgiving let your requests be made known to God" (Philippians 4:6).

The method outlined in this verse for casting out anxiety is fourfold: prayer, supplication, thanksgiving and just telling God what you want. When you are worried, stop thinking emotionally and talking in an anxious manner, and pray. Ask God to relieve you of your fears and show you how to handle the problem that causes the fear. Then, immediately upon asking Him, give thanks, thus expressing your belief that He is answering your prayer, for He is.

"If you sit down, you will not be afraid; when you lie down, your sleep will be sweet" (Proverbs 3:24). It is important when dealing with worry to go to sleep at night in the right manner. If you retire with a mind filled with fear thoughts you will have only superficial sleep, for beneath the surface, anxieties are disturbing you in the deep subconscious. Therefore when you lie down to sleep think of God as being with you and watching over you. Place the cares of the day in His hands. Every night say this verse to yourself before you go to sleep. Then, instead of fears in your subconscious, faith in God's presence will develop a confident approach to your anxiety.

HOW TO SUCCESSFULLY MEET A CRISIS

What shall we then say to these things? If
God be for us, who can be against us?

–Romans 8:31

This topic—how to successfully meet a crisis—is not in any sense theoretical or academic. One does not need to be any great authority on human nature to know that there are scores and scores of people who at this very moment face crises. I know that because it is my privilege and function as it is of all clergymen to deal in human problems week after week, year after year. One who does not engage in this work can scarcely understand or perhaps appreciate the tragedy both potential and real that is constantly faced by human beings. We are a sophisticated people and it is characteristic of sophisticated people to dissemble. Their faces or their outward demeanor or actions do not show the intense suffering, conflict and pain that often lie behind apparently imperturbable faces. We have learned that you never need to be surprised at anything you may hear, at any problem that may be laid before you.

One day last week may well serve as an illustration. In quick succession I conferred with three persons. The first was a man about sixty years of age who had lost a position of responsibility that he had held with his company for many years. He was totally unprepared to search in the open employment market for a position. He felt that he was trained only for this particular type of work. His whole life had caved in upon him a day or two before. The second case was of a woman who had discovered the infidelity of her husband, admitted by him. She was dazed, bewildered, oppressed; her whole future was in jeopardy. The third was that of a man who faced one of the most intricate and difficult problems ever laid before me for counseling. If he decided one way he might be right, if he decided the other way he might be right, and if he made a mistake, so it appeared at least on the surface, it would affect his family in ramified ways that were astonishing. This is just a sample of what goes on every day. So many of the people I talk to face problems just as acute in one degree or another as those I have mentioned.

The wisdom of these people is that they came to the right place—not that they came to me, because I have no particular wisdom, but that they came to the Church and Christ, the source and center of their Christian faith. In coming here they were not coming to a man; they were coming to someone who stands in their thought as a representative of God. They realized, however dimly, that the successful solution to their crisis lay in their Christian faith, and that their faith was where they would get the answer.

In the scriptural account of the hours and days leading up to the crucifixion of Jesus we see unfolding before our very eyes one of the most astounding and marvelous demonstrations of how to meet a crisis ever written in the history of mankind. I never fail to marvel at Him. Quite apart from the fact that He is the Son of God and therefore has divine character, the very fact that He was incarnated in flesh and blood and bore all that he had to meet demonstrates to us how we, too, may meet a crisis. He deliberately set His face to go into this crisis. He did not dodge it. He took leave of his mother knowing that He would never see her again in the flesh.

He was cynically treated as a political football. There was no justice in His trial. He faced injustice calmly and I always think of Him when I hear a lot of people say that they do not know why they should have to face injustice. He did: that is all there is to it. So must we. His friends deserted Him. One of them betrayed Him with a kiss of affection to make it all the worse. They put a crown of thorns on His head and spit upon Him. They sneered at Him and reviled Him. Finally they loaded upon His shoulders a great heavy cross and drove nails through His hands and through His feet. All of that He withstood.

Incidentally whoever in the realm of art started picturing Jesus as an esthetic, weak type of personality certainly never read the Scriptures very well, it seems to me, because only a person of enormous vitality and powerful physical strength could have stood this. Here was a man in every sense of the word. It was hard to beat the breath of life out of Him; He was healthy in body, mind and soul. And through it all there was never a moment when He was not the Master. Old Pontius Pilate, a shrewd political schemer who knew a man when he saw one, took a look at Him and said,

"Ecce Homo"—behold the man. Jesus Christ had the astonishing genius of showing us how to meet a crisis.

What was His secret? If we learn His secret we can then apply it in our own crises. And His secret was this: At all times and under all circumstances He never had the slightest doubt that Almighty God was with Him. He knew always that He could draw upon the Divine resources. Always He was saved by the Divine presence.

A long while later one of His greatest followers caught it up in a sentence that holds the secret of meeting crises. Get this sentence in your mind and wrap it around your heart. Fill your soul full of it, and whatever crisis comes to you in your life, you can successfully meet it. This is the sentence: "What, then, shall we say in response to these things?" What things? Why, anything! Disappointment, frustration, nervousness, despair, anxiety, injustice: "What shall we then say to these things?" Well, the answer is…"If God is for us, who can be against us?" Isn't that wonderful? That is resonant, that is sturdy, that is the essence of victory. If anything bothers you in a crisis—your husband been unfaithful to you; your wife been unfaithful to you; you've lost your job; your Board of Directors has not treated you fairly; your associates have been unkind to you; you have been sneered at, lied about, mistreated; you are frustrated; you are hopeless—just take a look at Him.

"What, then, shall we say in response to these things?" They do not have any power. How do we know they do not have any power? Because the everlasting Almighty God is with us. Who or what can stand in the presence of God! That is the secret of meeting a crisis: a profound, undeviating, childlike, naive, sincere faith in the fact that Almighty God is with you. If you get that, you can go out of that church door and nothing at any time can defeat you.

Now what does it do for you, when you know you have God with you? In the first place it gives you the first factors in facing a crisis, and they are calmness, imperturbability, quietness. If God is with me, why do I get excited? I will not get excited; I will keep cool. In a crisis there is always one thing you need and that is your head. Almighty God gave us heads. There is not a person reading this book who does not have a head. The main purpose of a head is to eat with, smell with, hear with and, perhaps most importantly, to think with, but you cannot think when you are excited. Why can't you think when you are excited? Because the purpose of the brain is to receive and send messages, and when you are excited it is like everybody rushing into a reception office at a large company and saying, "Send a message here, send a message there, send a message there." The telephone operators would give up in despair and no messages would go out. The brain is a large reception desk.

When crisis comes some people become very confused and excitable because they suddenly feel desperate and they do not know what is going to happen. Instead, just say to yourself, "It might be worse. God is with me. I shall keep calm, and soon I will be able to say to all these things, 'If God is with me, who or what can be against me?'"

I believe in this calm and relaxed approach to crises. I try to practice it myself. I had an amusing experience the other night. A man told me that he had had a pseudo-nervous breakdown and was very nervous and excitable. I met him at a banquet at which he was the presiding officer. When he introduced me to the audience, his introduction ran something like this: "I am about to present to you the speaker of the evening. He has been of great help to me. I have been so nervous that I could hardly sleep, but awhile ago I bought his book and I put it by my bedside, and before I read half a chapter I was sound asleep." (Laughter)

After the first shock of this introduction I got to thinking, if the book gave the poor fellow calmness and quietness it was worth what he paid for it. When you face a crisis, just stop. That is the first thing you do, stop. Stop physically. For if your body keeps on moving your mind keeps on moving. Stop physically. Sit down, lie down, or, better still, kneel down and say—"Lord, you are with me and there is nothing on earth that is strong enough to defeat Thee. I put the problem in Thy hands." And when you get calm in your mind, your mind will begin to take on insight, illumination, intimations of the truth, and out of a well-ordered intellectual process you will get the answer to your crisis. "What shall we then say to these things? If God be for us, who can be against us?"

A second element in meeting a crisis is to practice the techniques of crisis-meeting that lie in the New Testament. Religious faith is not a helter-skelter proposition; it is scientific. You can go to the New Testament and find a scientific formula or answer for every human problem. I make no exceptions. By studying the New Testament you will become after a while an expert in crisis management. Scattered through it like nuggets of gold are little, simple formulae that may be applied in given situations. It would take a year or two of preaching on this theme alone to exhaust every one of them that is there.

In the late 19th and early 20th centuries, there lived a man named Charles Proteus Steinmetz, one of the greatest and most remarkable scientific men this country ever produced. He's most remembered for helping to establish alternating-current electricity. He said that someday religious teachers were going to establish Christianity as a science in meeting the problems of life just as skillfully as natural science did in its field.

Let us just take one for example, one in which I personally have great confidence. When a crisis comes up turn to this passage in Matthew 18:19-20: "Again, truly I tell you that if two of you on earth agree about anything they ask for, it will be done for them by my Father in heaven. For where two or three gather in my name, there am I with them." Is that to say that if I am in a crisis I should decide on a good spiritual friend to whom I can go? If you are in your business office and crisis comes up, ask that question. If it is in your home and crisis comes up, ask that question. If you are alone and the crisis arises, ask that question. And then go to a person with whom you believe you can share a confidence and ask him not to advise you particularly, but to pray with you, to join his prayers with yours on the basis that where two are gathered, God is also present. It is forming a combine. It is a three-way spiritual partnership—with God in the center. Just why this is so I am not sure, but much of life is a mystery. We know prayer works powerfully.

A man called me up one day and he said, "I heard you talking about that passage in the Bible where if two should agree as concerning a certain matter, that the Lord would help them in their trouble. Do you honestly believe that?"

"I certainly do."

"Why?"

"I do not know, only that I know it works. I do not know why I can pick up the telephone and talk to you as I am talking to you now. Why do you ask?"

"Well, I am in a tough spot. Now, we are not together. I am several miles from you. Does this spiritual law work over the telephone?"

"In the days when these things were written, there were no telephones. We do not need to be together physically. If we are together in mind, that is all that is required."

"All right, here is my problem. I am going to state it to you." He stated it, and it was a business problem. It was about ten o'clock in the morning, and he said, "Will you start praying with me (note, he did not ask me to pray for him but with him), praying that I will get an answer, praying that I will meet this situation."

"I will pray with you throughout this day," I replied.

"All right, I will talk to you later." So saying he hung up. That sounds very curious, but it was most sincere.

Later, he called and said, "Keep it up, it's got to work, and remember we are together in a spiritual partnership."

"All right," I replied. "I'm praying with you."

Along about four o'clock, he called me up again, and with happiness in his voice said, "Shut off the power. It is going fine. Everything is good."

I have a feeling the Lord would like this man. "Shut off the power." It was perfect faith.

"What happened?" I asked.

"Why," he said, "after talking with you this morning I got calm and quiet, sat down here at my desk, and I began to think. And I put the matter in the hands of God, and I got a feeling that God was right here with me, and I began to have a feeling of confidence and power and mastery. I just put myself in God's hands and I got the answer to my problem, that's all."

I have another friend who is one of the greatest intellects of this country. He is a very distinguished personality. He wrote me a letter and said, "Please pray with me in a very serious crisis through which I am passing." I did. I met him a few days later for lunch. When you see this man walk into a place he is master of all he surveys, a dominant, great, stocky individual to whom men defer because of the great quality of his personality. I saw him that day as a kind of a scared child with an awful crisis resting upon him. So I told him the story of this man and "shutting the power off."

When we had finished our lunch, he said, "There is no place around here to pray, so let us pray right here."

So I reached over and took him by the hand and repeated the Scripture passage, "Again, truly I tell you that if two of you on earth agree about anything they ask for, it will be done for them by my Father in heaven. For where two or three gather in my name, there am I with them." And I said, "You and I together are putting this matter in the hands of the Heavenly Father. Now leave it there. Have faith and trust that it is going to come out, that it is going to be solved."

I'd be glad to share with you a letter I received from this gentleman soon afterward. It read, in part: "The power is on and always will be."

What then shall we say to these things, the things that bother us, that create "crisis." Enumerate them. List them in your mind now: one, two, three, four…Got them in your mind?

"What shall we then say to these things? If God be for us, who can be against us?" He will make you calm so that every element of your mindfulness strives for a solution. There is a friend of mine who came to me and said, "I have sat in your congregation time and time again, and I have heard you say these things and try these techniques. Not long ago I got into a crisis and I went to a man who said to me, 'Why, you are afraid, aren't you? Why don't you put this in God's hands?'" He did, and this very morning he came to me telling me that he has been helped. This is not theoretical. Practice your faith along this simple line and you will find that Jesus Christ has indeed demonstrated the power to successfully meet crises.

ON TEMPTATION

The moral problem is not that we have temptations, but what we do about them. As an old saying has it, we can't keep birds from flying over our head, but we can prevent them from building nests in our hair. Temptation, in one form or another, attacks each of us. But fortunately we have spiritual weapons for gaining victory over it. One is the following verse:

"No temptation has overtaken you that is not common to man. God is faithful and He will not let you be tempted beyond your strength, but with the temptation will also provide the way of escape, that you may be able to endure it" (1 Corinthians 10:13).

This assures us that no temptation will ever come that has not been faced by others. And if others were able to overcome it, so can you. Moreover, God will not allow any temptation to attack you that you are not able to overcome. That is a very constructive thought to hold in mind. No matter how strong a temptation may be, it is not beyond your strength; you have the inner power to defeat it. God understands the problem of temptation and has given you a way out. God is faithful, He will not allow you to be tempted more than you are able to stand, and along with the temptation, He provides a way out and encourages you to conquer it.

"Let the wicked forsake his way, and the unrighteous man his thoughts; let him return to the Lord, that he may have mercy on him, and to our God, for he will abundantly pardon" (Isaiah 55:7).

Temptation is a moral challenge that develops in our thoughts. Therefore, to overcome temptation, simply think right until your thoughts are good thoughts and not bad ones. Then you will have the power to stop wrongdoing and return in thought, purpose and dedication to God. When one does this, he receives forgiveness and pardon.

"He has sent me to proclaim release to the captives and recovering of sight to the blind, to set at liberty those who are oppressed" (Luke 4:18).

People who are the victims of recurring temptation through their weakness are indeed "captives." They fully understand what Charles Dickens had in mind when he said, "I wear the chains forged in life." The worst prisons are not made of iron bars and stone, but of thoughts. We imprison ourselves by our wrong thinking. But when we repent and surrender ourselves to Christ and want freedom, He sets us free.

WHATEVER YOU DO, DON'T STOP GROWING

And the child grew, and waxed strong in spirit, filled
with wisdom: and the grace of God was upon him.

–Luke 2:40

A "youngish" doctor was being considered for an extraordinary
medical opportunity. I employ the descriptive word "youngish" to
mean a bit beyond young but yet not old. He was a brilliant man,
with a most engaging personality and was immensely popular.
His bedside manner was notable. He was one of the best golfers in
town, and at a cocktail party he was the life of the occasion, so they
say, but he did not get this great opportunity. He was bypassed by
a man obviously inferior as to mental agility but much more substantial in character and in scientific achievement.

By way of explanation, those making the selection declared
that the more brilliant man did not get this position because he
had not read a single medical book since the day he graduated, nor

did he read any accredited medical journal. He never turned up for the medical convention and he had never written an article for a learned society. The eminent physician who told me this story solemnly said the reason he was passed by was simply because he had stopped growing. He was standing still. He reached his peak and would henceforth go into the process of retrograde. Whereupon this physician shook his finger at me and said, "Whatever you do, don't stop growing for one minute."

When a man has stopped growing he always reveals it by some such statement as this, "That is not the way they used to do it." You want to know how old a man is in his ideas? Analyze him to see if he gives you that reaction. Or he may say, "That is not the way it was done when I was a boy."

I recently met a "down east'er" from Maine, who was thinking of joining one of the great churches in New York City, but after some evaluation he decided he would not. When I asked him why, he said that he did not like the way they do things. They do not do things in a great, well-established church in New York City as they did in the church from the man's youth, some forty-five years ago in Maine. It's not as though one church is inherently better than the other; it's that this man was so accustomed to what he knew that he was giving up on having fresh, interesting experiences.

Whatever you do, don't stop growing. Examine your emotions, examine your ideas, and if they have begun to crust over smash them by a spiritual renewal. A friend in whom I have great confidence told me that in his town a woman bought a car that she brought back to the dealer after several months complaining that there was something wrong with it. She could not get it go over thirty miles an hour. The mechanic was astonished but took the car out and found it would do everything that was claimed for it—sixty, seventy, even seventy-five miles an hour. It was almost unbelievable, but upon investigation he found that the woman had never learned to shift from second to third gear.

Now don't you laugh: if I told the absolute truth about myself, I wonder whether I have ever shifted from second to third gear mentally, emotionally and in terms of the spirit. Take a good look at yourself. What could we be, what could we do, if you and I arrested this terrible process of stagnation and stimulated the process of growth.

Of course, Christianity teaches this truth. Every year we celebrate Christmas, a birth. If you read the Gospel according to St. Luke, you will see that immediately when he finishes with the Christmas story, that is the birth story, he begins to tell you a growth story. The next paragraph after the completion of the Christmas story and the incidents pertaining to it deals with Jesus at twelve years of age. First, St. Luke tells us about the birth of the child. The next thing he tells us is that the child grew and increased in stature and in wisdom and in favor with God and man. In other words, the message of Christianity is: after birth comes growth, increase in physical stature, increase in wisdom, increase in spiritual stature.

Obviously, when you apply this problem to society, you at once face an appalling situation. Every year we celebrate Christmas. But perhaps we ought to have a second worldwide celebration to consider growth, for the disparity between our technological development and our spiritual growth is utterly tragic. It has been commented upon by wise men for long years as they have observed it. We have become very advanced in the realm of scientific knowledge and the application of the forces of nature to our common life, but we are still living in the kindergarten of spiritual understanding.

Now here is a Book that is quite interesting. You read in this Book about Sodom and Gomorrah, about Nineveh, about Tyre, about Babylon. They were civilizations that were destroyed. Why? Simply because they went bad. I read an article once about the famous Johnstown flood of 1889 in Pennsylvania. Interestingly, what I remember about the article is the portion that discussed what do people do when they are told that some great disaster is about to come down upon them. Some men in Johnstown that afternoon were counting their money, some men in Johnstown that afternoon were examining their goods, some men in Johnstown that afternoon were taking pride in their homes, but the word came: "The great dam has burst, run for your lives, run for the hills." Everybody left everything and ran for the hills and watched the great surging waters inundate the city of Johnstown. And we have seen as much in our biblical studies as well. Run for the hills, the hills of God: you will find refuge there.

I suppose there is no experience in the history of a human being so marvelous as when he is reborn, when a man who had stopped growing once again begins to grow. We have a mechanism for that in Christianity: We are born and then we are reborn. You could not help being born the first time; you had no control over it. But the second time a man can determine to be reborn and when he is what a change comes over him. I have been asking myself, as I think every individual should ask himself, here I am at this stage of life, am I any better than I was twenty-five years ago or am I worse? Have I grown petty in my thoughts? Have I grown uncharitable in my attitudes? Am I kindlier or am I a meaner man than I used to be? Do I still dream dreams and see visions? Am I still moved by lofty impulses or have I grown cold and cynical? Have I stopped growing or do I progress? Those are solemn questions. Many a man who has this wonderful experience of rebirth describes it so ecstatically that I can believe it is the greatest experience of life.

I was in a little town in Ohio where I was speaking. I was to take a forty-mile bus trip back to a city where I was staying overnight. A middle-aged man came up and offered to drive me in his car. Scarcely ever have I talked to anybody whose conversation was so sparkling and exuberant. Finally I said, "You are so exuberant, so happy, so effervescent, you talk like a person twenty-years of age. Of course you are much older than that. How old are you?" "One," he answered. "One what?" "One year." "Oh, plus how many? Do you mean fifty-one?"

"I mean one. I lived for fifty years but I was old and miserable and tied up inside of myself. About a year ago, I experienced what you preachers call a rebirth. It is amazing how wonderful life has become. So I say I've really lived only one year."

"What happened to you," I asked, "to so completely renew life?"

"I simply found Jesus Christ, that is all. He touched me and He made me over. I was reborn and now I live so completely that I am starting life all over again. I am now a year old."

That is the secret. Grow in the spirit and life will be perpetually new. Whatever you do, do not stop growing.

ON DISAPPOINTMENT

When you are in the mental gloom of disappointment, some straight thinking is called for. Disappointment can cause you to be so emotionally disturbed and depressed that you will be unable to think effectively. As a result, you cut off the creative forces that are ready to help you the minute you are able to be helped.

Disappointment is a prevailing and common adversary of the human spirit and may strike you almost anytime. Therefore one should learn to deal with it. Four verses can be of great help in so doing. "Therefore, do not throw away your confidence, which has a great reward" (Hebrews 10:35).

When disappointment strikes, simply hold tight to your confidence. Do not petulantly toss it away. Instead, affirm. I am confident. I believe. It will require some mental and spiritual effort to maintain confidence. Your tendency may be, in desperation, to toss it. So focus your mind by an act of will on confidence. The promise of the text is that such practice will bring great reward. "Bless the Lord, O my soul and forget not all his benefit" (Psalm 103:2).

The practice of thanksgiving is a great viewpoint changer. Add up all the benefits you possess. This wise verse tells you to start thanking the Lord for all the benefits He has given you, instead of mentally, and perhaps vocally, harping on what you glumly believe has been denied you....Be content with what you have; for he has said, "I will never fail you nor forsake you" (Hebrews 13:5).

The word contentment derives from two Latin words, *con* and *tenere*, meaning to hold together. When you have faith in God, your mind will hold together so efficiently that you can always recover from a disappointment. Thus you can be content and, out of contentment, great things can happen. "We know that in everything God works for good with those who love him, who are called according to his purpose" (Romans 8:28).

When disappointed, try loving God all the more. Carefully analyze yourself to make certain you are thinking and living in harmony with His spiritual purpose. It could be that you are off the spiritual beam. Instead of dwelling upon the word *disappointment*, think of it as "Hisappointment." What you regard as a disappointment may actually be a wonderful new appointment or plan for your life, namely, His plan.

Always take a positive view toward disappointment. It could be that through disappointment you are being shown another way or being led toward something different. If you have tried sincerely and prayerfully, and things have not gone well, then look upon disappointment as an opportunity to ask whether you should move under God's guidance in another direction.

LIVING AT PEACE WITH YOURSELF AND OTHERS

Thou wilt keep him in perfect peace, whose mind
is stayed on thee: because he trusteth in thee.

–Isaiah 26:3

A certain businessman has always impressed me by his calm and peaceful manner. I asked him how he managed to find inner peace, how he learned to live in peace with other people. He declared that the formula is a simple one. He made the positive assertion, which he obviously believes, that "everything in the Bible works." At least he never found anything that did not work. He told me that his personal discovery of living at peace with himself and with others is in a statement from Isaiah, a text that is an old favorite of mine: "Thou wilt keep him in perfect peace, whose mind is stayed on Thee." That is to say that Almighty God will keep a man inwardly at peace and in harmony and goodwill with his neighbor when he fixes his thoughts, not only on the low level of fear or incrimination or antagonism, but habitually upon God. "Thou (said Isaiah) will keep him in perfect peace, whose mind is stayed on Thee."

The formula is obvious. The trouble with us is how we think. When you put that formula into practice, when you keep your mind stayed and fixed upon God and His great strength and quietness, rather than upon the nervous apprehension of your responsibilities, you begin to have peace and quietness inside. One thing you learn not to do is to become anxious. One must learn not to be rigid or to overstress. Then he will become relaxed, quiet, spiritually pliable. It is remarkable how many people break themselves today simply because they are so drawn up on the inside, so tied up.

Someone told of a blacksmith who was putting a steel rim on the wheel of a wagon that was to be used on concrete pavements. This man asked the blacksmith how long he thought those steel tires would last on paved streets. The blacksmith replied that, since they were of the finest quality steel, they ought to last for three thousand miles. (I suppose it would take a wagon a long while to go three thousand miles.) He then talked with a tire salesman and asked how long rubber tires on an automobile would last. This salesman was apparently an optimist, for he thought those tires ought to last for forty or fifty thousand miles. Becoming more conservative, he said they would last at least thirty thousand miles. In other words, an inflated rubber tire will last ten times as long as a steel tire. The steel tire goes crashing along hitting every obstacle straight on, while the rubber tire is pliable; it fits into the nooks and crevices, it has give and take, it has inner easiness, inner ease.

This serves to explain why some people break and some do not. A man gets spiritual pliability whose mind is stayed on Thee.

Great athletes possess this quality. I have watched athletes across all sports and I have never seen a great one who did not have inner ease. A batter never made a record who approached the plate with an attitude of rigidity. It is easiness, the released attitude, that brings results.

That is the way one lives when he is at peace with himself. Don't allow yourself to block your strengths by worries and anxieties. Get your mind up above those things, get your mind on God and say to yourself, "All the power and force I need to meet any situation will flow to me from Him if I keep myself yielded to Him, if I keep my mind as a transmission mechanism fixed on Him." The spiritual life is a very great art. It is a pity that so few have learned the subtleties of it.

A second way to have inner peace and outer peace is to practice keeping the mind stayed on God in relation to other people. How do you achieve the most with other people? Certainly not by antagonizing them, by resisting them, by saying, "I will show them."

You and I get mad at people, do we not? We do not like them. We go around with grudges in our hearts. Often we do not know why, but we just don't like them. Sometimes it's simple: We do not like the way they dress or the way they talk. They get on our nerves, they rub us the wrong way, so we pick at them. Then we wonder why we have no inner peace, and we wonder why we have no outer peace.

A woman told me she used to be "mad at everybody all the time, beginning with her husband." She lived in a constant state of madness. She was madder at some people than others. One day she came to meet with me and we decided on a plan whereby if she did not like somebody, she was to pray for them. But she rebelled at this for a while, saying she believed all of the Bible except that. That, so she thought, was a "foolish theory." It would not work; it was impractical. She wanted spiritual power, she wanted inner peace; she wished to know how to get along with people. Finally she adopted the suggestion and started praying for people.

Later she reported the result: "I came to the day when I really wanted to get mad at somebody, but, strangely enough, I did not seem able to work up a good mad feeling toward her. In other words, I found my angry feelings getting away from me. Finally I realized the ability to get mad had gone."

What was the answer? She had been keeping her mind stayed upon God and His great, sound, practical principles of human living, and so she just could not get mad any more. She had inner peace and peace with others.

What I am stating here is the simple principle by which a person can have inner peace and outer harmony. I am not delivering any theoretical, high-sounding, poetic, philosophical discourse here—that is obvious, you know that without my telling you—but I am laying down three simple principles for inner peace and peace with God and man. First, keep your mind stayed on God and live in a relaxed attitude. Second, keep your mind filled with prayer for people who irritate you.

And third—this is even simpler than anything else yet said—if you honestly want inner peace and if you want to be in harmony with God and man, then see to it that the thing which destroys this peace is eliminated. The thing that keeps people teetering through life, that makes them nervous, irritable, irrational and contentious, more times than one would believe is just plain wrongdoing in their lives. I remember a few years ago, a man came to see me one day. A big, fine fellow who walked up and down my study and said, "How does one get peace? I am so nervous, I cannot sleep. I'm continuously fighting with my wife and the people in the office! Life is one series of conflicts after the other."

"Have you seen your doctor?" I asked.

"Yes, I have been to see him. He has taken cardiographs and everything. My heart action is a little fast and my blood pressure is up. The physician says all I have to do it quiet down, but I cannot quiet down."

"That is too bad. Why can't you quiet down?" I asked.

"That is what I want you to tell me," he replied.

After prayer and discussion, I asked, "You have not done anything wrong, have you?"

"I want you to understand, I am a respectable citizen of my community," he snapped.

"Do not shout it at me," I suggested, for when one shouts a denial there must be some doubt about it.

"Why would you insinuate such a thing about me?"

"I am not insinuating. I am merely asking you. You came here as to a kind of spiritual doctor, and if you want spiritual treatment you have to lay yourself out on the operating table. That analysis is necessary if we are to know what is wrong with you."

"Well, it is like this," he started to say slowly. "I siphoned off money for quite a while. I handle the books, and I had the chance and I siphoned a little off extra beyond what my employee paid me."

"How long have you been, as you say, siphoning it off?"

"Ten years," he replied.

"You must have quite a little sum siphoned off by now."

"I have, but I do not have it all."

"What did you do with it?"

"I spent some on my daughter's education. Some went into the purchase of a home."

"Does it make you feel better to tell me that?"

"Yes, it does."

"Have you ever told anybody before?"

"No, I have not, but I feel better already. Now, what am I going to do?"

"The first thing you must do is to ask the Lord to forgive you." He did this with great earnestness.

I said, "You must take the first train and go back down home and make complete restitution."

He did so, accepted his punishment (which is not as harsh as you might imagine, being that he came forward of his own volition) and now he not only has peace of mind and lives in harmony with himself, but he actually has more money today than when he was living in dishonesty. If you want inner peace and the calmness that enables you to live in harmony with your fellow men, simply get right with God. Stop doing wrong, start doing right. And there is no better time to perform this process than right his very moment. You shall have peace. Trust in God.

ON COURAGE

Have not I commanded thee? Be strong and
of a good courage; be not afraid, neither
be thou dismayed: for the Lord thy God is
with thee whithersoever thou goest.

–Joshua 1:9

I wish to give you a sentence of few words but of tremendous power, which, if received and retained in your mind, can give you courage to overcome every difficulty. You may question whether words can accomplish so great a result, but you must never minimize the creative force of an active idea. A mental concept has more voltage than electricity; civilizations are changed by ideas. Was it not Emerson who said, "Beware of an idea whose time has come"?

We have in my church a woman who has been extraordinarily successful in the institutional care of children. Over a period of time she has adopted the practice of approaching the children who are most neglected and have developed a feeling of inability, and every night just before they go to sleep she says something courageous to them. Her theory is that courageous thoughts planted in their minds just before they go to sleep will lodge deepest in their consciousness. She has observed these children and reports that, in a remarkably short time, their IQs have been raised by fifteen to twenty points.

Now it would not hurt some of us to have our IQs raised, but that is not the function of this book. But we do need to have our courage raised. I am going to give you a sentence, and if you will open your mind to receive it and will conceive of the thought as dropping from your conscious into your unconscious mind, it can, in due course, raise your courage until you are sufficient for every difficulty. These are the words: "Be strong and of a good courage; be not afraid, neither be thou dismayed: for the Lord thy God is with thee whithersoever thou goest." That comes from the first chapter of Joshua, the ninth verse. When you go home, I wish you would write those words down and say them over and over to yourself, for courage is an absolute necessity in this life.

I have in my pocket a Swedish proverb taken from Amos Parrish's magazine. As a matter of fact, I think this proverb is enough to give you this morning: "Fear less, hope more; eat less, chew more; whine less, breathe more; talk less, say more; hate less, love more; and all good things will be yours." You will notice the proverb states, "Fear less." In other words, get more courage. How do you go about doing this?

First, you must practice courage. I can only repeat that which I have often said. In athletics, if you want to succeed, you practice. To be a good musician, one must practice. Why do we assume that we may become expert in the spiritual realm without practice? If you are filled with fear, you probably have practiced fear for so long that you have become expert at it. The secret of courage is to practice courage. Set yourself daily to thinking courageous thoughts. If there is a situation in your life that fills you with fear, endow it not with threatening qualities but with beautiful ones. Think it into an advantage to you, an asset. A psychiatrist had for a patient a little girl who frequently dreamed of being attacked by a tiger, so that she shrieked in terror. Upon investigation he discovered that an angry cat had once sprung at her, and later, in a zoo, she had seen a tiger. Asked to describe the tiger of her dreams, she said he had a big white spot on his forehead and stripes all round him; big red eyes and big teeth and it snarled at her.

"I have seen that same tiger," the psychiatrist told her. "You have the wrong idea of him. He isn't a mean old tiger. He is a great, big pussycat, and he wants to play with you. If you will notice, his claws are not showing. They are drawn in because he would not hurt a little girl for anything in the world. You think he is snarling, but that is his way of smiling. If you will look deeply into this tiger's eyes, you will see that he is kindly. Anyway, he is not a tiger, but just a great, big old pussycat. Next time you see him, say, 'Hello there, big old pussycat,' and you will love him."

Well, the little girl had that quality that, God help us, most of us do not possess—that of wonder. Next time she encountered the tiger in her dream, though she shrank back at first, she said to him, "Nice tiger, come play with me." She learned to like him and did not dream about him again. That story is right out of a scientific laboratory.

Do your tigers spring at you at night? A man wakes up in the night with a little pain, which he imagines is a heart attack. Probably it is not that at all. Look your tiger in the face. Say to yourself, "I think my heart is all right. I put my heart in the hands of the Lord." It is how you think about such things that is important. Practice thinking courageous thoughts. If you are really in earnest about getting courage, go through the Bible and copy down on cards every statement you find that has to do with courage, and every day commit one of them to memory. When you find a sentence in the book you are reading that fits your need, commit it to memory. Fill your mind with these thoughts. With your mind filled with courageous thoughts there will be no room for fear. I know this works for I have tried it on myself. It requires great willpower because we are more at home with our fear-thoughts. Charles Dickens said, "Men love their chains." That sounds ridiculous, but it is a fact that we grow to feel comfortable with the fetters to which we are accustomed. We even take a certain comfort in our miseries. If you are a victim of fear, you must say to yourself, "I will practice this idea of putting courage-thoughts in my mind."

I met a man the other day who taught me something. The plane that was taking me to a city where I was to make a speech was late in arriving at the gate. I ran through the airport and out to the cab stand carrying my heavy bag.

"Taxi?" asked a man, and when I nodded, he grabbed my bag and put me into his cab. "I saw what you did," he reproached me, "running up those stairs two at a time, and at your age. You ought to have more sense!"

"What do you mean, at my age?" I protested. "I'm not puffing, am I?"

"Fellows like you are dying like flies of heart attacks. I know, I carry them around. They work so hard to get somewhere that when they get there they keel over. What's the use of getting there if when you get there you can't stay?"

"That sounds like logic," I agreed.

"These men ought to practice calmness," he continued. "They are victims of tension. If they'd learn to be quiet they'd live longer and be happier. Nobody should worry about anything. Worry's bad for them. A lot of people have what I call the worry habit. They ought to break themselves of it."

"My friend," I said, "you are a philosopher. It is a pleasure to talk to you."

I guarantee on my honor that what follows is the truth. This cabby began to quote statements that I myself had made. He quoted me word for word. "Where did you get these ideas?" I asked him.

"I read them in the daily paper," he said. And he gave my own name as author of the column I had been writing for the newspapers.

When I paid my fare I told him who I was, for though I may have given him ideas, he had given me what I am now trying to give you. He was a rough kind of fellow, but when I went away I think I shall never forget the happy, glorious look on his face as he said, "Remember now, you can give yourself peace and power and live a long while if you just let these things soak into your mind."

One of the great things about preaching is what you get back from the congregation. Anybody who thinks preaching is an act where a man stands on an elevated structure and hands down wisdom to the people, telling them to do this and do that, has a wrong concept. Preaching is a laboratory experience; the preacher gathers techniques of life and submits them to other technicians in the laboratory, meaning the congregation. They in turn put them to the test and report back to him. One says, "This technique works beautifully and while I was working at it I found another."

"Good," says the preacher. "Let me test it in our laboratory." And before very long, the preacher and his congregation have built up a body of spiritual practices that will enable anyone to overcome any difficulty. Practice, then, thinking courageous thoughts, and the greatest thought with which to begin is the text, "Be strong and of a good courage; be not afraid, neither be thou dismayed; for the Lord thy God is with thee whithersoever thou goest."

Then there's the second part of the Scripture: "For the Lord thy God is with thee whithersoever thou goest." God is with you wherever you go and under whatever circumstances you may be living. If you will believe that, and practice it and yield yourself to it—it makes no difference what obstacle or difficulty you have—I now assert without fear of successful contradiction, you can overcome anything in this life. We are told you will not be tempted above that which you are able to withstand; that you can rise above every difficulty. Lawrence of Arabia said, "There is nothing man cannot stand." Once, when beaten by the enemy with whips until he thought he could stand no more, he found new reservoirs of power and was able to say to them, "Lay on! I can take it." If a human being has within himself these deeper levels of fortitude, so does he possess tremendous powers for overcoming his difficulties. And if he believes in God and practices the presence of God on the basis that God is with him under any circumstance or condition, then I tell you he can have courage to overcome anything.

I am going to illustrate. We are about to publish in our magazine *Guideposts* one of the most thrilling and remarkable stories that has come to my attention in years. This story has been given the glorious title, "By Wheelchair to the Stars." You don't often go to the stars by wheelchair, do you? But this man did. At the age of seventeen, he was seized with rheumatic fever. Complications set in, and severe arthritis. The mere wearing of his clothes was torture. He cringed when a window shade flapped. At seventeen he was finished, through, useless. The word "useless" cut into his mind more painfully than the nerve ends that so tormented him. His father and mother were textile workers; that left him sitting at home alone all day in a wheelchair that his father had made, suffering excruciating pain in body and mind. But he had the good old American spirit, the manhood that has always characterized our people. He wanted to learn. He wanted to do something. Somebody suggested that he could illustrate greeting cards—he had a decent artistic talent. Not a bad idea, but that wouldn't thrill you, would it? But he said he would try. He worked six months to make a card that sold for a dollar. His hand became so crippled he could hardly use it. Just when he thought he was making progress and had gained a certain self-confidence, he had a bitter experience. He slipped and fell out of his chair about eight o'clock one morning and lay on the floor, helpless, for hours.

He tells the story in his own words: "I couldn't rise. I struggled and sweated and wept with impotence. And on the kitchen floor I battled again the wave of black bitterness that I'd only recently conquered. Hours passed. If I ever prayed in my life, I prayed then.

"Eventually, the mailman came on his late-morning round. Our mailbox was outside the kitchen, and when I heard him come I yelled for him. He came in and picked me up. And we chatted. I just wouldn't let him see how humiliated I felt. So I got to joking to hide my feelings."

"Harry," said the carrier, "you've got what it takes. I wish I had your courage. Where did you get it?"

"I haven't any really," Harry replied. "What little I've got came from a Book where it says, 'With God nothing is impossible.'"

During the next year Harry made eight thousand dollars from selling his greeting cards. He began selling them through the mail and word-of-mouth. The family put a mortgage on the house, borrowed some more, and bought twelve thousand boxes of assorted cards to retail for one dollar! "If you don't sell them, what then?" asked his mother. "With God nothing is impossible," Harry answered.

He sold not twelve thousand, but *nineteen* thousand! His mail-order business continued to grow, and he says, "I will never forget the first time I realized that I had done a million dollars worth of business."

Now Harry rides in a plane, which he flies himself. He has even learned to play the Hammond organ. He plays the melody with one finger of the right hand and fills in the harmony with the left hand, supplying the bass with one fairly good foot. He concludes this article, "By Wheelchair to the Stars," by thanking God for the terrible struggle he has had and for the pain God, in His wisdom, gave to him. And he thanks God that he has found the greatest secret in this life, which is, "With God nothing is impossible."

Remember this: you can go to the stars by wheelchair. You, too, my friends, with your little troubles and your big troubles. This is a fact, worked out in the laboratory of Christian Experience.

"Be strong and of a good courage, be not afraid, neither be thou dismayed." Practice that. Why can you be sure of success? Because in the glorious concluding line it says, "for the Lord thy God is with thee whithersoever thou goest," even though it be through the darkest shadows in the world. Always have courage, over all difficulties.

HOW TO REST IN A RESTLESS AGE

Come unto me, all ye that labour and are
heavy laden, and I will give you rest.

–Matthew 11:28

It is a pathetic human fact that with all our knowledge and materialistic achievement we Americans really do not know how to rest in a restless age. A few days ago, if I may use so prosaic an illustration, I was seated in a barber shop. A fine-looking man of about forty or forty-five years of age came in and took a seat beside me.

He slumped down rather dejectedly, gave a long sigh and said, "I don't really need a haircut, but it's worth the price to have a few moments of complete rest. I push myself so hard, become so fatigued, that I cannot think very well."

After a pause, he added, "Frankly, I don't believe I know how to rest any more."

We need to learn the art of resting for our physical and emotional good, and in order to grapple efficiently with the problems of our time. Christianity has always taught expertness in the art of resting. Don't get the idea from this that we provide services of worship where you can go to sleep. Christianity is not serenity, nor is it something soft and comfortable. Christianity is rugged—there is fight in it. You can hear always in Christianity the sound of trumpets and see the waving of banners. It summons people to high moral struggle and endeavor. But it helps them do that by first teaching them how to rest. In its emphasis on rest there is a universal appeal.

Dante, the great Italian poet, came one evening to an old monastery and asked shelter for the night. The monks gathering about him asked where he was going and the purpose of his journey.

He quietly replied, "I am searching for that which every man seeks: peace and rest."

Men struggle, they aspire, they have ambition, they achieve, and there is a great thrill in pitting oneself against life, in realizing its highest attainments. But all men have their times of dreaming, and their dreams are of peace and rest. They are dreams of softly splashing water down green banks; dreams of the sea washing softly on white shores of sand; dreams of old grape arbors by a back door; dreams of bending fruit trees in the sweet haze of an Indian summer; dreams of light whispers of the wind amid tall and ancient pine trees; dreams of peace and rest, all of them. There is something in the stately spire of a church that points men away from the confusion of life to the eternal quietness of God. There is something in the pulpit of a church that forms a bridge between this world and another. There is something in the melody of the words of the Scriptures falling upon human ears and lodging deeply in human hearts that heals the tension of men's lives.

I spoke to about fifteen hundred men in the ballroom of a great hotel. There had been a great deal of drinking beforehand, and it was a noisy, rough, tumultuous situation. I had been invited to speak on "Practical Techniques for Reducing Tension." These men needed that. I worked around at them for a few moments with some so-called jokes, trying to break down the barrier that always exists between a minister and such an audience. The mere fact that you are introduced as a minister means "two strikes" against you before you start. You have to establish a rapprochement between yourself and the audience. I began to quote a few passages of Scripture dealing with peace and quietness. You might think that would be the worst approach possible, but in the choice of Scripture passages I was fortunate. I recited a verse that I consider in many respects the most beautiful sentence ever composed: "Come unto Me all ye that labor and are heavy laden and I will give you rest." I saw the strange effect it began to have, and repeated it twice, three times. Before it was repeated for a third time there was a death like hush in that hall, an indescribable peace filled the room touching those hard pressed men like magic. It was an unforgettable moment as if some other hand took over. One other passage was from Exodus where God, in encouraging Moses to do a very difficult thing, said, "My presence will go with thee, and I will give thee rest."

In those words is the essence of the secret of resting in a restless age. Get fixed in your mind, driven in deeply, the idea that God's presence goes with you to give you rest, and you will master the art of resting.

How does this mental reaction help you to find rest?

First, because, in some profound way, this relieves the mind of stress. We do not get tired in our bodies nearly so much as we get tired in our minds. One sinks into a chair saying, "I'm so tired my very bones ache." But your bones do not really ache; often the ache is in your thoughts, which desperately seek relief from strain. The mind should learn to rest as it works. If one has a calm faith in God's presence, believing that He provides help, one may live with quiet energy, one automatically draws upon deep resources of power.

Power is derived from quietness, for quietness administers rest and renewal, together with the ability to think clearly. Carlyle spoke wisely, "Silence is the element in which great things fashion themselves."

I take occasional speaking trips. One reason I do this is because by getting away one can get work done. People think a preacher lives in some ivory tower retiring in stately dignity to work in peace, far removed from the world's turbulence. He is supposed to preach two or three sermons a week, and sometimes I think the best way to do it is to go away into some far-removed, quiet place.

Curiously enough I have found that one of the quietest places in this restless and turbulent age is a seat on an airplane. Unless you happen to meet some talkative friend who fastens himself upon you, it is possible to shut yourself in and work undisturbed to your heart's content. I almost feel that it might be to my advantage and, incidentally, to the best interests of the Church, if along toward the latter part of every week I took a long trip on an airplane. Perhaps my sermons would be more quickly accomplished and the result more satisfactory.

All of which is to say that a few days ago I was on a plane taking a rather long trip to fulfill a speaking engagement, and in my seat was working on a sermon. I was working hard, perhaps too much so. When I started to block out the outline I thought it would flow easily and simply, but it did not. I sat at the tray table with my pencil poised for a long time, staring at the paper but without writing down a syllable. Strenuously I thought and sat. The hours went by, and with dogged determination I said, "I will finish this sermon before I go to bed tonight if I do not go to bed at all," which, of course, is wrong way to try and get things done. The best method in such an impasse is to break the tension. Break your tension by reminding yourself that God's presence will go with you and give you rest.

Another technique of resting in a restless age is one suggested by my friend and fellow pastor William L. Stidger, namely, to rest wherever you are. You do not need to go to Atlantic City to rest, as much as I like Atlantic City; nor need you go to Florida, as pleasant as is a trip to Florida. You can rest right where you are. You can have a perpetual sense of God's presence as constantly giving you rest. For example, at this moment, I am working on writing this book, yet I am pausing and resting. The greatest figures in our national and business life are people who know how to rest where they are.

One of the most indomitable characters we ever had in the United States was William Jennings Bryan. He was one of the greatest orators ever to arise among us. There is scarcely a town in the United States where Bryan did not speak. He did not have the benefit of quick transportation. For the most part he had to use old branch line trains, even freight trains. I talked with a friend who as a very young man accompanied Bryan as a reporter on a campaign trip. He said that "Bryan wore them all out." At three o'clock in the morning he might have to change trains. That did not bother him; he seldom took his clothes off, but had the ability to slump down in his seat and accommodate his body as best he could to the hard seat, and fall into a deep untroubled sleep. After ten or fifteen or twenty minutes, he would be wide awake. Then, for hours on end, the grueling program of speech after speech would leave him unperturbed. It was not only his ability to sleep anywhere that saved him. It was also his strong sense of the presence of God that afforded him the power to relax and draw new strength upon which to live his strenuous life. He knew how to rest where he was.

Another simple suggestion of resting where you are is while waiting at a traffic light to offer a brief prayer, thus using that interlude for meditation instead of exhausting energy by nervously honking your horn. It works, as I know from personal experience. What would happen if, every time a light changed, every taxi driver, bus driver and motorist in the city of New York had a minute of prayer? I really believe that such practice might help solve New York's difficult traffic problem. Somebody somewhere is going to make himself immortal by suggesting how to solve the traffic problem in this city and perhaps this is it. Let everybody pray a little prayer when he has to stop in traffic. If this practice should not completely solve the traffic problem, it might at least result in having fewer nervous people in New York.

Rest where you are and for as long as you can. Practice now letting the tension and the strain go out of you. Do that the next time you're in church and you will walk out of that church door with a wonderful sense of rest, your mind quieted, your nerves eased. The tension will go from your body and mind and a deep peace will be in your soul. You will have discovered one of the important reasons for going to church, namely, to learn how to rest in a restless age.

Listen to these healing words, themselves an effective therapy: "Come unto me all ye that labor and are heavy laden and I will give you..." Do not struggle nor strive for rest; He will give you rest. You are relaxed at this moment, you are quiet, deep within. God's presence broods over you, therefore turn to Him in your thoughts and He will give you rest: "My presence shall go with you and I will again give you rest."

Fill your mind daily with the affirmation of the presence of God, the cool, quiet, vast presence of God. Say confidently to yourself, "God is with me, He is giving me peace and rest, I shall not be nervous or tense." By such practice, you shall acquire skill in the very great art of knowing how to rest in a restless age.

ON CRITICISM

You will be criticized if there is any righteousness whatsoever to your personality. There is just one way to avoid criticism: Never do anything to amount to anything. Get your head above the crowd, and the jealous will notice and criticize you. Therefore welcome criticism as a sign that your life has vitality, as a confirmation that you're accomplishing things.

"Actually a critic is an asset (though at times an unpleasant one) for he keeps you alert and causes you to study yourself. Bless those who persecute you; bless and do not curse them" (Romans 12:14).

This wise, though admittedly difficult, advice will really work in dealing with criticism. When anybody criticizes you, instead of criticizing him in return or fighting back with him or saying unkind things about him behind his back, simply bless him. Ask God to help him. Pray for his well-being and that his life may be filled with blessings. If you follow this procedure, your critic— instead of receiving opposition from you, which is destructive— will receive goodwill, which is creative and life-giving. You may not win him over by blessing him, but you will remove the sting from yourself and possibly help him overcome hatefulness. "Repay no one evil for evil, but take thought for what is noble in sight of all" (Romans 12:17).

There is always a tendency when criticized to repay in the same coin. Something evil has been done to you. The old "Adam" in us all wants to give evil in return. But that only makes the whole situation more evil. And it is a simple fact that no good ever comes out of evil. So this verse tells us to do what is noble. When you act small, it is bound to react unfavorably to you. But when you do the noble thing, the big, generous and righteous thing, criticism of you will fail in its intended purpose because everyone will see that the criticism is unwarranted.

"Beloved, never avenge yourselves, but leave it to the wrath of God; for it is written, 'Vengeance is mine, I will repay,' says the Lord" (Romans 12:19).

It is not our business to get revenge. That is the prerogative of God. It is He who repays people for wrong they have done, not you. He does not allow us to exercise vengeance and thus set ourselves up as judges and punishers. He alone is the judge of men's actions. He punishes where necessary. So leave it to Him for He can do it better than we. And besides, He does it constructively.

Never answer a critic, keep your spirit right. Learn all you can from your critic; honestly analyze and correct yourself where necessary. Thank him for his input but do not let him cut you down in action or in spirit. It is easier to criticize others than to look within oneself. "Why do you look at the speck of sawdust in your brother's eye and pay no attention to the plank in your own eye?" (Matthew 7:3). Remember this verse when criticized. I find it most helpful to remember when I'm getting ready to return fire. Bless your persecutor, then go on doing your job to the best of your ability. That is all He requires from us.

WE CAN HAVE A GLORIOUS FUTURE

From there he went up to Beersheba. That night
the Lord appeared to him and said, "I am the God
of your father Abraham. Do not be afraid, for I
am with you; I will bless you and will increase the
number of your descendants for the sake of my
servant Abraham." Isaac built an altar there and
called on the name of the Lord. There he pitched
his tent, and there his servants dug a well.

–Genesis 26:23-25

One of the most tragic things that can happen to an individual or
to a country is to lose faith in the future. When this occurs you can
be absolutely certain that a sad process of deterioration and decay
is in effect. On the contrary, no matter how many difficulties may
be faced, either by an individual or by a nation, if there remains an
unshakable faith in the future, one saving element is present that,
despite everything, can guarantee a glorious future.

When I was a boy, which I assure you was not too long ago, nobody had the slightest doubt about the future of the United States or the world. Every day, glorious achievements, marvelous new inventions were announced; men were dreaming dreams and seeing visions; we were coming into the golden age and everybody was filled with the spirit of expectation regarding the future. Every school-aged child was educated on the proposition that great days were ahead. Nobody had a pessimistic outlook. It was a mood of optimism and growth. Then we had a war and a long depression, then another war. Then somebody discovered nuclear power. Now people fear a third world war. Of course, in view of all this it is not difficult to understand why a mood of depressive cynicism rests upon the people.

I find myself now and then longing for that glorious, effervescent, uplifting mood of yesterday. Apparently I am not the only one. I read not long ago in a southern newspaper a very interesting and, I think, wise article pointing out that there are so many historical novels today. Historical fiction is constantly on the bestseller list and is one of the most popular types of reading we can find today. This newspaper writer says that two facts account for this interest. First, the American public is utterly disgusted with the no-count kind of people found in the average novel. Second, we are aware of the sad state in which the world finds itself, and there is a general feeling on the part of the people that in order to have a glorious future we must go back and discover what those great old Americans of yesterday possessed that we have lost. Hence the popularity of the historical novel.

We, the sons and daughters of those people who believed in a glorious future and who created the same, want to discover what they had that we lack. The Scripture quote at the beginning of this section refers to a large passage of Scripture about Isaac, who was a man of genius. He discovered, as he came into a glorious country, that the wells that his father Abraham had dug, and out of which had poured pure fresh streams of living water, had been allowed to be filled up by the Philistines. Isaac, longing for the greatness that was in his father Abraham, redug the old wells of water that they had dug in the days of his father Abraham. When once again these pure streams ran free, then was discovered the ancient power of the old days. That is an allegory so simple that a wayfaring man, though a fool, need not err therein. We have had a host of Philistines today who have clogged up the wells. And we have allowed them to do it. They have come along with their attitude of super-sophistication. They have come along with their slow but steady hacking away at Christian morals. They are still at it. On the best-seller list today are books which make it very easy for anyone to think that there is such a lack of morality in the United States that we might just as well throw everything aside and become the kind of generation that was blotted out when Vesuvius threw its lava and ashes over what was apparently one of the worst communities of the ancient world. The walls of great living are filled up by the Philistines, and no wonder there is no flowing of the streams of water that alone can make us believe in the future. People have become indifferent to the great moral values and are cynical, soft and forgetful of Almighty God. They are fiddling while Rome burns, while civilization decays.

When you redig these ancient wells out of which the creative future bubbles, what do you find? Simply, that the people who created great futures in the past were strong, decent, self-sacrificing, idealistic people. The men and women who created these United States were great souls. They did not play both sides of the street. They formed their convictions on what they thought was right and they let the chips fall where they would. They did not have a lot of little politicians with their ears to the ground, figuring to balance this minority group against that minority group. I do not know whether this democracy can stand that kind of business or not.

I was at Mount Vernon recently and was greatly moved. A strong, courageous man once lived there. You can see his footprints everywhere; you can get his spirit. This great, tall, silent Virginia farmer, of a fine family, believed in something. He went out from that place to lead a ragged army of untrained men against the mightiest power then known to history. They were poor and hungry and without food, but they were dreamers of the future. One day while Washington was away, according to a letter that I saw at Mount Vernon, a British warship came up the river and trained its guns on Mount Vernon. A messenger came ashore under a white flag to tell the overseer that unless they, Mount Vernon, contributed food for the British vessels, the plantation house would be blown up. The overseer had been charged by Washington with the care of this magnificent property. He was in a great dilemma. He pondered seriously over the matter and, finally, fearful for the plantation property, he gave them food and whatever they asked. Then he wrote to Washington about it. He said, "General Washington, we gave them food." Washington's reply showed his sterling character. He said, "I love every inch of Mount Vernon. It is my home, and the retreat to which I hope to return when this war is over.

Now I am with my troops and we are fighting to build a future; I would rather you had allowed the enemy to lay waste my manor house and destroy my plantation than to give them any aid or comfort. I am ashamed of you, Sir!"

That is the kind of people who made the United States, and that is the only kind of people who can save it. People of strength and character, just plain, simple, unadulterated, old-fashioned Christian character and manhood.

Take the story of the Great Wall of China as another example. For fifteen hundred years it stood unconquered. Enemies came up against it, they hurled great armies against the wall, they brought up catapults of fire, they smashed at it with battering rams, but they could not break the wall. One day, by the gate, a guard was drunk, and a simple, harmless-looking shepherd came along and engaged him in conversation. Realizing his drunken and maudlin state, he corrupted and bribed him. The guard went away from the gate for a moment; it was thrown back and hordes of barbarians poured in. They could not overcome China by bringing force against the wall, but they gained entrance by penetrating a man who had grown weak.

Keep yourself alert, keep yourself strong, keep yourself decent, keep yourself Christian, for you are the soldier at the gate guarding the future of the United States. No wonder Isaac redug the wells of water that they had dug in the time of his father Abraham.

The second thing that we need to redig is a new emphasis upon the morality and Christlikeness of the home. The basic unit in America is still the home, and with it the institution of marriage and of children. What we need is for mothers and fathers once again to bow their heads before meals, as did their fathers and mothers, and ask the blessing of God upon the food, the home and each member of the family. We also need to revive some of those beautiful and gracious old-fashioned American customs of morality that made up a great people. Let children see their fathers and mothers reading out of the Great Old Book of God.

I have a friend who was formerly quite a sophisticate. He believed in making money, and he thought the opportunities in the free enterprise system were limitless. He asked me one time if I thought it was unchristian for him to strive hard to build a good business and a nice home. I said that I never could see any reason why a Christian should not improve his own condition, provided he does it decently and in harmony with the laws of God. I told him to build himself as good a house as he could. So he finally moved into a beautiful home. But the crowd around him was a fast crowd, and he saw what was happening. He wrote me a letter the other day and said that in his new house he found the most magnificent bar you ever saw. All the neighboring houses had bars. But when he took his children through the house and they came to this room they asked, "What is this, Dad?" I said, "That is a bar."

They then asked, "What is that?" I replied, "Don't you know?" They said, "No." Then he says, "I removed the bar and on the shelves where whiskey bottles used to stand, I have put the greatest books I could find."

Now you say, how in the world can a man do that and be in society, because to be in society you have to follow the mode. Who said you have to follow the mode? Young people come to me again and again and say, "I have to follow the crowd." I do not know much about social etiquette, but I think Miss Emily Post is an authority. Somebody wrote Miss Post a letter that was in the newspaper. Dear Miss Post, "We do not drink in our home and we wonder if we have another couple in to dinner if we must serve cocktails the same as everybody does. Also, what about serving drinks after dinner." This is Miss Post's reply: "You do not have to serve liquor at any time."

This deterioration of the American home is an enemy in the gate. This sentiment I just quoted from Miss Post is not popular. You know that. Do not get the idea that I think liquor is the only bad thing in this country. It is a symptom, it is a let-down. Let me ask you this. Are you as good a man as you were forty years ago? What are your children going to do, what are mine going to do? Before I go to my long-last sleep free from the cares of this world, I would like to say, with Daniel Webster, "When my eyes shall be turned to behold for the last time the sun in heaven, may I not see it shining on the broken and dishonored fragments of a once glorious Union." But rather let them gaze on a strong Union of strong-limbed, clean-minded, healthy, soulful people. Unless we have it, there is no future; it will be one with Nineveh and Tyre. Let us redig the wells that were dug by our forefathers in their time.

ON ANGER

It is very important what you do when angry. Your action rides, to a large extent, on the destiny of your life. You can stir up trouble, make enemies, ruin chances or make yourself sick. On the contrary, by proper handling of anger you can keep situations under control, cement friendships, win respect and stay healthy. I suspect that some people's lives have been ruined by anger. By the same token, the skillful mastering of anger has added to the effectiveness of many. The following verses constitute an extraordinarily effective anti-anger technique: "Good sense makes a man slow to anger, and it is his glory to overlook an offense" (Proverbs 19:11).

This verse pits good sense against anger and stresses the value of imperturbably overlooking offense. When anger surges upon you, just say to yourself, *It is stupid to get angry. It won't get me anywhere except into trouble. The momentary satisfaction of letting go isn't worth the difficulties I will experience as a result.* In this manner, you may talk yourself into being sensible. This rational procedure will slow down your anger-reactions, and help you rise above the provocation. In other words, meet anger with urbanity.

"Know this, my beloved brethren. Let every man be quick to heat, slow to speak, slow to anger" (James 1:19).

This verse teaches us to be alert to people and situations but always to react slowly to emotional stimuli. The longer you can keep quiet the more effective will be your reactions. Don't say the sharp words, do not make the quick retort, do not write that nasty letter—or, if you do, tear it up. Say nothing. Keep quiet. Make no rejoinder. Practice the great strategy of delay.... "do not let the sun go down on your anger" (Ephesians 4:26).

Never let a day end without getting rid of your anger. This advice is psychologically very sound. Empty anger out every night to keep it from accumulating. In your prayers drain off any anger content that may be in your mind. Forgive everybody and practice the great art of forgetting. You can build up resistance to anger by letting these verses soak into your thought processes until they exert an automatic check upon your emotional reactions. Study them. Memorize them. Use them.

STAY ALIVE AS LONG AS YOU LIVE

The thief cometh not, but for to steal, and to kill,
and to destroy: I am come that they might have
life, and that they might have it more abundantly.

–John 10:10

Recently one of the youngest men of my acquaintance, a remarkable person, drove me around his city. At times I thought I would never live through it. Then he wanted to show me something, and we had to walk. The walking was worse than the ride. I soon found myself breathless, and I resolved that henceforth I would associate with people my own age. This energetic gentleman is eighty-four years old. But it is not his physical vitality that impresses me so much as his eager interest in life. Form and color have an immense appeal for him. He called my attention to and commented on the beauty of sunlight on the trees and on an old stone church. For him everything in life has charm and fascination. At eighty-four he is alive to his fingertips.

When I mentioned it, he said, "I am going to stay alive as long as I live." This sentence caught my fancy, and ever since, I have been debating the question: can one stay alive as long as he lives? Deterioration in life is always facing us; the burden of our cares tends to take the zest and keenness of existence from us; our minds close up; we circumscribe the area of our interest; we do not read; we do not think; we do not participate in the mental exercise of significant conversation. We die on the vine. If we were not walking around showing some sign of activity, the undertaker would certainly get us. There are many people who are dead but do not know it.

In them is none of the exuberance of living. Half-starved, they go into drug stores for vitamin tablets, trying to build up some efficiency in the body. The word "vitamin" means life-substance. Thousands upon thousands of these half-starved people want to live, but they have not developed within themselves the capacity. Christianity offers life to everyone. Most of us have some Christianity; some of us have a great deal. You can generally measure the degree by how completely the old deadness has departed. Life is the gift of faith.

I recall going to western Pennsylvania to speak at a convention of young folks. I did not have any idea what I was to encounter. My first feeble remark had a semblance of humor and was met with a roar of laughter. Either I am becoming very witty, I thought to myself, or these young people have never heard anything funny before. I then told one of my best anecdotes, and I tell you I never had such a reaction in my life. It was wonderful! That audience challenged me; they were way ahead of me and forced me to depths within myself. After it was over and they were asking questions, I said to one boy, "You are all young; you are all happy and eager. Why?"

"Don't you know?" he replied. "We have had our lives changed."

The reason the Christian religion has lived for twenty centuries is because it satisfies the basic longing of people everywhere toward life. I realize that you go into many churches and do not see much life; everyone is solemn, gloomy, as if at a funeral. I doubt if Jesus would recognize that kind of place as a Christian church. The Bible says again and again, "Rejoice in the Lord always: and again I say, Rejoice." That is what Christianity does for people. Jesus said, "I am come that they might have life, and that they might have it more abundantly."

When you get this life in you, you stay alive to the end of your days. And I do not believe you stop living even then. Men like my eighty-four-year-old friend go bounding into heaven, stirring things up over there. Stay alive as long as you live.

When that vitamin, the spirit of Jesus, gets into your existence, what does it do for you? It makes you live as long as you live. It takes away one of the greatest deterrents of life, namely, self-centeredness. If I put myself in the center of all my thoughts, I commit personality-suicide. Self-love, self-pity, self-interest are, physicians tell us, destructive maladies. They cause personality to wither and die. You have to get away from yourself. Why this is so I am not sure.

Ask God to take out of your mind these constantly accumulating thoughts about yourself. As long as you have a place to sleep and food to eat and a job to do, forget yourself and start loving other people; and you will live. There is a couple I have known for a long, long time. The first time I met them they had asked me to have dinner with them. "You are always telling about people who are radiant," they said. "So when we heard you were to speak in this city, we thought we would try to see you. We want to live; we want to be that way; but we have no such reactions as you describe. We go to church occasionally." "How occasionally?" I asked. And they had quite a debate, determining which Sunday they had been to church. "Of course you read the Bible every night before you go to bed?" I asked.

"Well, no," they answered. "We have a Bible, but we don't read it."

"How much do you pray?" I next inquired, and it turned out that they didn't pray much either. Then the conversation turned back upon themselves: how much money they had, their social relationships. As I got to know them better I discovered that they were highly critical of other people. When I was to speak in their city again they were extremely indignant that they were not seated at the head table at the dinner that followed. Then something happened. The husband wanted a promotion in his business. I knew he was figuring on it, though he said nothing to me about it. The next time I was in town they telephoned me and came to the hotel to see me. He had not been given the job. Some little "whipper-snapper" had it. The man didn't say much, but his peppery wife expressed for both of them what she would say to any of the board of directors next time she had the opportunity. And she asked if I didn't think she was right.

"No," I said. "You are not firm enough. If you are really going to talk to them, you should tell them what you think. Let us have a rehearsal. If you hate them so, go through with it, live it out.

Don't mind me." Thus encouraged, she made a work of art of it. When she had finished, I said, "Now leave it with me." "Oh!" she exclaimed. "Will you tell them?" "Just leave it with me," I repeated. "You have cleaned it out of yourself." Then she saw what I was driving at. "All right," she said. "But what would you do?"

"If I were you, I would get away from myself. The trouble with you people is that you are always thinking about yourselves. That is why you are miserable. Let us pray for this man who has the job. Let us thank the Lord that he got the job. Let us promise the Lord that you will help him all you can, that you will keep on at the same job you now have and cooperate with this man." She looked at me, her lips in a straight line. "I am not going to talk to the Lord that way. I just can't do it. If you want to promise that for us, I will listen." Then her husband spoke. "It is sensible," he said. "I will pray." And he prayed.

He prayed for the man and he prayed for the board of directors. I used to visit that city frequently, and I noticed that they had grown quieter, different. I discovered that they had broadened their interests and activities. One day the wife met me in the lobby of my hotel. "I am speechless," she exclaimed, which was a remarkable situation. "What do you think? The young whippersnapper we told you about has been sent to another city, and Bill has his job."

There are people up and down the country who say that Christianity is theoretical. Had this man told the board what his wife told me there in my hotel room, he would have been fired. But when they began to practice love, to become interested in something outside themselves, the man grew to a stature that brought him his promotion. This wife used to tell me at great length about all her aches and pains. Now she is healthy, happy and alive—all because she and her husband got outside of themselves. I could labor this point. You know whether you are tied up within yourself. Get interested in things and people outside yourself, and you will live as long as you are alive. There is something else, what we might call an emotional and spiritual malady, which keeps people from living: people are ill in their thoughts, ill in their emotional responses, ill in their souls. How can you live as long as you're alive if you are ill in your soul?

I was reading a book the other day about the effect on the body of emotional dispositions. It told of a woman who developed arthritis every time she visited her son-in-law. When she got home from the visit, the condition cleared up. (There is no record about how the son-in-law felt.) A man who was cheating on his partner developed asthma. The feeling of guilt caused these reactions on the body. A friend of mine, a writer, called me on the telephone one day. "Norman," he said. "I am in pain. I've got to see you." And when he came he elaborated, "I do not sleep; I am dull and stupid. And the thing that bothers me most is that I cannot write anymore. But I have to write or I will die! It is my whole life; it is the expression of myself."

"What other symptoms do you have?" I asked. "I feel all tied up; I am dead on the inside." Then the story came out: infidelity, one sin after another. He sobbed, "Why did I ever get myself into this? I can't look my wife in the face, or my sons. I am afraid of them. Everything is closing up on me." If I ever heard a man tearing himself to pieces it was this man. And I let him do it. This is what causes people to live lives that are living dead. And I am not overstating it either. Well, we got him free, and he is healthy and happy and brilliant today. The old words flow off his pen and the ideas out of his mind. We are all the same, every one of us. We will fight for life to the last gasping breath. And the only way to stay alive as long as you live is to have love in your heart and purity in your soul. "The soul that sinneth, it shall die." When you come back to God, get healed and recreated, the color comes back to your cheek, soundness to your heart, light to your eye, spring to your step. Dark shadows fade away. It is morning again. This is the way to stay alive as long as you live. "I am come that they might have life, and that they might have it more abundantly." Take it; it is offered you. Do not miss it. It is what you want; it is what you can have.

ON SUCCESS AND FAILURE

And as Jesus passed forth from thence, he
saw a man, named Matthew, sitting at the
receipt of custom: and he saith unto him,
Follow me. And he arose, and followed him.

–Matthew 9:9

Some time ago I was traveling with a friend whose mind is occupied almost continuously with one question. He seeks information on that subject from nearly everybody he meets. "Why is it," he asked, "that some people succeed while others fail?" Then he related instances of unlikely people succeeding and likely people failing. His definition of success is mine also, as I am sure it is yours. It is not a matter of money. We have all known people who have made money and been successful in life. We have also known people who have made money and been personal failures.

Nor is it true that the people who get their names in the paper are necessarily successful. I do not need to labor that point. What my friend and I mean by success—and I am sure you do, too—is the ability to do things better than well. It is the faculty of releasing your own greatest potential; of possessing a calm and peaceful mind; of utilizing that mind to its maximum; of having satisfactory personal relationships; of doing something useful in the world. Above all else, it is the ability to get along in harmony and peace with yourself. Broadly speaking, it means making the most of oneself. Curiously enough, while we were having this conversation on the train, a young man spoke to me. He had heard me speak in the city from which I was returning home. He sat down and talked with us. Then my friend asked his question.

"Let us make me the guinea pig for the moment," he said. "I am one of ten children born in a hillbilly family in the southern mountains. My father and mother and all ten of us were illiterate. The others still are, but I got out. I love them and respect them, but I live in another world; and so, I am afraid I have lost them and it troubles me. But I could not have done differently. Something was tugging at me all the time. I had to leave; I wanted to be somebody; I wanted to do things. I did not want to eat what they ate, talk as they talked, dress as they dressed; I wanted to make something of myself. The impulse came one night in church when the preacher told what Jesus could do for human beings. I knew right then that I had something within me that had to be released."

That, of course, is one of the great contributions of Christianity. I never speak before a congregation that I do not feel the tremendous romance of what people can be. What can I be? What can you be? Perhaps you are middle-aged: what difference does that make? You may be old, and yet your greatest accomplishments may come in the sunset of your life. Remember: the birds sing most sweetly at sunset. Never lose the thrill and romance of what you may be.

That is Christianity, and it is all tucked into one Bible verse. It is the autobiography of Matthew and, incidentally, is an illustration of writing skill. Study the Bible for its economy of words, for saying so much in a brief space. "And as Jesus passed forth from thence, he saw a man, named Matthew, sitting at the receipt of custom: and he saith unto him, Follow me. And he arose, and followed him."

That is the entire story. There was old Matthew, a tax gatherer: gold running through his fingers, liking the feel of the money, scanning his ledgers to see where he might squeeze out a little more. All of a sudden a shadow fell across his book. He lifted his head to see a man looking down on him in a kindly fashion. The eyes looked him through and through, and in that glance Matthew saw his destiny. Jesus said to him, "Follow me." And Matthew closed his ledger, got up and followed Him. But he took with him his pen for the book he was to write—one of the masterpieces of the ages, The Gospel According to Matthew. One of the great factors in the Gospel According to Matthew is that it contains a secret for everybody that, if cultivated, leads from failure to success. And what is this twist or slant that makes the difference? I would say that, first of all, it is necessary to get an obsession. There are good obsessions and there are bad obsessions. Get into your mind the obsession that humbly, and with God's help, you are going to succeed in life, that there is no power in this universe that can make you fail. A wise man, Lord Halifax, said, "Failure and success are habits." That is true. Some people form the habit of failure. They just know they are going to fail; they think failure; they insist on failure. If you argue with them, they reply, "You may be right; but you don't know me." They might as well answer, "I'm going to fail no matter what you say." I know this is true. I have sat in conference with people who build a wall around themselves, or to change the figure, they are an island where there is no place to land. They defeat every attempt to reach them with a constructive idea.

They have what's called "the will to fail." They may want to fail to spite someone. The mind plays curious tricks. Lord Halifax goes further. He says, "If you hold a thought long enough, that thought will take you prisoner." That is a terrible sentence, terrible because it is true.

Hold the thoughts of defeat and failure, and they will take you prisoner. I have no doubt there are people who are the prisoners of such thoughts. On the other hand, positive thoughts with God's help, will give you such power that you can do what you want to do. Let that thought take you prisoner. Get positive, objective, definite thoughts into your mind.

This is one of my favorite themes, and my business is to preach sermons. I have not preached my ideal sermon yet, but I am going to, one of these days. I can see that sermon ahead of me, urging me on. I tell myself that the day I preach it I will retire. But I won't. I will be back the next Sunday trying to preach a better one. I was in Miami the other day. It was nice down there, really nice. The sun shone all day and at night the moonlight through the palms fell like silver on the rippling water. I tell you there is nothing like the balmy, salubrious climate of Miami. I made a speech there and then had to go to Palm Beach, about seventy miles away. A prominent businessman offered to drive me. He was an experienced driver who knew the road. When I got into the car I asked this gentleman his business. He was an undertaker, and I had a most interesting conversation with him.

"How did you get into this business?" I asked.

"I always wanted to be an undertaker," he said. "A really good undertaker can do a lot of good in the world. People turn to him in their dark moments just as they turn to their doctors or their lawyers or their minister. A man who has dedicated his life to taking people to their last resting place in a Christ-like manner is never forgotten.

"It is a great and honorable profession. When I was a young fellow, I got the idea that if you begin to think in terms of God and human service, and believe that God will help you, and surrender your life and your job to Jesus Christ, you will be a happy man."

There are people who think of nothing but their own weaknesses or other people's weaknesses; their minds are filled with gloom; they see nothing but failure ahead. Do you know what you need? Get yourself converted. People who get drunk or run off with someone else's wife or steal money are not the *only* sinners. Another kind of sinner is the man who does not realize the greatness and dignity and tremendous power of his own self. Get a vision of yourself, what you really are. Then look up and see that Great Figure; look into His eyes; hear Him say, "Come, my son, my daughter. Come away from all this. Follow me." Let the word of God penetrate your mind; cast aside your negative thinking and let faith into the control center of your being. If you do that, tremendous things can happen.

There isn't an individual in this world who needs to stay as he is. Open your mind, open your heart. Take Jesus Christ in and all that He means. Until you do, you have not realized your own potential and how to release it.

I stand on a pulpit every Sunday and say that; I have a great soul within me. I was not meant to be defeated by anything. I have been in the house of God where I have been told in the name of God that I can be what I want to be. Put your hand in His. Believe in Him. Let that thought take you prisoner, and that thought will set you free. That is the romance, the mystery, of why some people fail and some people succeed. The result depends on the kind of thoughts that take you prisoner.

ON PRAYER

Pray without ceasing.

−1 Thessalonians 5:17

I do not believe there is the slightest doubt that the prayers of human beings get results. This faith is not based on religious considerations alone. I would prefer to say it is the result of prolonged laboratory experience. Over the course of a good many years I have been compiling prayer-results of hundreds of people. The results are astonishing.

"Prayer is the greatest power in the universe," says a great scientist, "and," he adds, "it is a pity more people do not make practical use of it."

More and more people are using prayer. A notable Southern businessman says, "This is the prayingest generation that has ever lived. The curious thing is," he adds, "that you do not need to go to church to find people who pray. A lot of praying is being done by people you would never suspect of it."

Would you expect to find groups of businessmen praying in the financial district? "No," you say, and you would be wrong.

You will find such meetings in such places as the Chamber of Commerce. Prayer meetings are being held by businessmen at noontime. Typical of this is a prayer group conducted by my friend Fred Rackliff, a hardware merchant in New Britain, Connecticut. He admits publicly that he was rather "off the beam" spiritually at one time, and he was upset that he was losing the business his father had left him. Then he had an experience of spiritual rebirth. Now every week he is a member of a luncheon group. During the meal they are as raucous as any men you could find anywhere. But after luncheon, conversation ceases, and they sit for fifteen minutes in meditation. Then someone breaks up the meeting with a prayer. The church of which Mr. Rackliff is a member, at one time only sparsely filled, is now crowded to capacity every Sunday.

A great many remarks have been made about the Congress of the United States; but do you know that every week a prayer meeting is held in the restaurant of the House of Representatives that had been attended during the last session of the eighty-first Congress by considerably over a hundred Representatives? I was there myself one morning when there were present some of the most distinguished political figures of our time. They were praying for what? For the legislative day, for themselves, for their enemies: Democrats, Republicans, all praying together. And in the Senate the same thing happens: a group of sixty Senators of all shades of political opinion meet once a week for breakfast to pray. Great industrial organizations in America are putting chaplains on their staffs. The Bristol Manufacturing Company of Bristol, Rhode Island, makers of shoes, employs a Baptist minister. He is to do good in whatever way he wishes to go about doing it.

A great many people just do not know what is going on today. They are amazed at the idea that anybody does any praying outside a church or his own bedroom. God is getting popular in this country. There is a man in Chicago who operates a health club. His name is Jack Smith, and his club is one of the biggest and finest in Chicago. He has written an article for the magazine *Guideposts* entitled, "God's Roughneck." That is what he calls himself, because he was at one time a prizefighter, then became a truck driver, and then a taxi driver. Finally he set up his health club business. He says that as he probes for physical flabbiness in his customers, he also looks for spiritual flabbiness because he believes you cannot get a man physically healthy unless you get him spiritually healthy.

What does that mean? One cannot go around praying *all the time*; you have to do your work. You cannot shut yourself in a room and get down on your knees and pray without ceasing.

You do not need to do that. The secret is to keep your thoughts filled with God. Whenever you think of it, at frequent intervals just say the word "God." That is all you need to do. That is a prayer. Or say the word "Jesus." Or just think about Him as you are on a bus or walking along the street. Think about God or Jesus. Say to yourself, "You are with me; I am with You. Your power is all around me, everywhere." To pray without ceasing is to keep your mind on God. We have to divide this subject into two parts. First, and this is very important, you must forget yourself and send out prayers of helpfulness to other people. A self-centered life is ineffectual. If you reach out to other people, pray for other people; enough of these prayers will cling to you to transform your entire life. Recently I met a very inspiring person, a man of about forty. When he was a small child his mother had left him on the front porch while she did her housework. Somehow he got to the edge of the porch and fell head over heels and hurt his spine.

From the age of twelve he has been confined to a wheelchair, and yet I found him one of the happiest men I have ever met. I had heard stories about people like that and had taken them with a grain of salt. Often the legend is built up out of pity. But as I sat with this man I suddenly became aware of the fact that I was feeling better myself. I felt happy and had a sense of God's presence. "You have attained a rare happiness," I said to him. "Yes, sir, I have," he answered. "I wish you would give me your technique," I said. "Oh, it is so simple you would never believe it. I just pray for people. That is all."

Lately I've been rereading one of the greatest books ever written, *Prayer, the Mightiest Power in the World* by Frank Laubach. He believes that you should go around every day praying without ceasing, using fractions of minutes to pray. He believes you can change the world by doing this. He has some curious methods. He will come to church, get in a back seat, and pray against the backs of the heads of everyone within view. He says the results are absolutely astonishing. People will turn full around and smile at him. Once he prayed against the back of the head of a sour-looking man sitting in front of him. Suddenly the man began to stroke the back of his head. Once on a railroad train he sat praying at the back of a woman's head. Suddenly she turned around and said to him, "What this country needs is more religion."

"Are you a missionary?" he asked, astonished. "No," she said, "I'm the wife of the conductor on this train."

"Why, then," he persisted, "did you suddenly turn and say to me that we need more religion?" "I don't know," she said. "All of a sudden I got to thinking that it was a good idea." Does that sound peculiar? I was sitting in the pulpit one day and I saw a face over near the wall. I could only see the profile, and I said to myself, "That is the face of a saint." Finally he turned and I recognized Frank Laubach. Prayer made him that way.

I have a method that I find most helpful. When I get up to talk to an audience I say to the Lord, "I love these people. They are all Thy children. Let me help them, won't You?" I was speaking at a Chamber of Commerce dinner in a large city. I saw a fellow scowling at me, or at least I thought he was scowling at me. Before I started talking, I said, "I love that fellow, Lord." And as I talked I was thinking about him, practicing some of Frank Laubach's prayer tactics on him. After the meeting when I was shaking hands with people, my hand was caught in a mighty grip and I looked up into the face of this scowling fellow, only he was smiling now. "Something touched me in your speech," he said. "The Lord touched me, I believe." It was not my speech: it was emanation of prayer that reached him. I have no doubt the day will come when we can prove these claims scientifically. Every one of us has in our brains and in our nerves thousands of little batteries. The human body's magnetic feeling has actually been tested. The human brain is sending off this power in its thoughts. It has been scientifically demonstrated that we have sending stations in us. But this goes deeper. There was a man with whom I had been working, an alcoholic, who had been "dry," as they say, for about six months. He had gotten out of my sight, and one day about four o'clock I had a strong impression that I could not shake off. It kept coming to me, so I started praying for him. I prayed for about an hour.

Then the impression seemed to let up, and I stopped. A few days later he called me on the telephone. "Norman," he said, "I have been in Boston and I'm still dry. But last Thursday I had a hard time." "About four o'clock?" I asked him. "Yes," he said, astonished. "Who told you?" "God did," I replied. "But tell me about it."

"I was in the Parker House and I got a whiff of the drinks as I was passing the bar. I had a terrific struggle with myself. I thought of you and said to myself, 'I wish Norman was with me.'" He did not have Norman with him, but he had God with him. His thoughts, sent toward me, got me to work praying for him. What did he do? He went into a drug store, bought a box of candy, went to his room and ate all of it. That seemed to be a good idea: candy and prayer. That got him over the crisis. We are living in a difficult time. Would you like to help the leaders of this country, or of any other? Do not doubt but what you can. Send spiritual power to them. When you read the President's name in the paper, send a fragment of prayer toward him. We know that there is in this universe an enormous force called prayer-power. Do not be a kerosene-lamp, horse-and-buggy individual. Spiritual power can change people's lives and the life of the world. Generate it in your prayers and send it out by a sort of radioactive prayer-power.

The second factor in this subject of prayer is that you have the right to pray for yourself. Everybody ought to pray for himself. Maybe we do not pray for ourselves properly. You will not fully get God's power by saying an occasional prayer in church. Fill your mind with God, fill your minutes with God, until you have developed all around you a spiritual magnetic power. All of a sudden, at a moment when you expect it least, marvelous things will happen to you; it is the result of praying without ceasing.

I do not relate many prayer experiences out of my own life, though I have them all the time. I regard this business of preaching as a laboratory process. I am simply one of the technicians in the laboratory. I outline in sermons certain experiments I have seen people working out successfully. I pass on their formulas to other people so that they can work them too. These people come back and tell me of their results and then I tell you. I met a man the other day when I was autographing books in a bookstore. He was carrying six books. He put them in front of me to autograph. Now, I appreciate anybody getting six books and so I thanked him, and he grinned. "Do you want to know who I am?" he asked, and put a card in front of me. I looked at it and I want to tell you that he certainly was somebody judging by all the things on that card. "When are you going to write another book?" "I don't know," I said. "I'm working on one, but it's a slow job." "I'll tell you what to put in your next book. Just say there is a tremendous power in prayer and faith that will change everything for anybody that lives by them." "How do you know?" I asked. "I've tried it," he answered. The truth of what he said was written on his face. "I hope our paths cross again," he said, as he picked up his six books. "When they do, I'll tell you all about it in detail. But I tried prayer, and it works. It is a scientific process that always gets results." I looked at his card again. He was a member of a scientific society. He had experimented, he had demonstrated. He knew. Such a man would not have had faith in something that did not work.

Live with God. Pray without ceasing. I will make you a proposition. Spend ten minutes of every waking hour in prayer for one week; pray without ceasing until this time one week from today. And I will guarantee you such power and joy in your life as you have never before experienced. Your prayers will get results.

HOW TO FIND GOD

But if from thence thou shalt seek the Lord
thy God, thou shalt find him, if thou seek him
with all thy heart and with all thy soul.

–Deuteronomy 4:29

The human personality needs refreshment. It has certain hungers that must be satisfied, and when they are satisfied you have a feeling somewhat similar—though on a higher level—to that experienced after finishing a delectable meal.

I recently had a curious and interesting day. Due to a series of circumstances arising out of an airline strike, I wound up having to take a train from Pittsburgh back to New York, the only transportation readily available. I groaned when, at eight o'clock in the morning, I got on my train and figured the number of hours it would take me to get to New York. I made all manner of uncomplimentary comments at finding myself in such a predicament. But it was a day I shall not soon forget.

As the hours went by I began to realize that there were no telephones, no conversations, no co-workers, no cell phones—a refreshing experience to contemplate eight hours without such minutiae. I had the rough draft of some articles and other manuscripts with me and spent a long time polishing and reshaping them. I worked on a sermon. I read a magazine article. All day I rode through mist-covered hills and deep, hazy valleys and singing rivers washed by sunlight. The hills, getting ready for the transformation we call fall, still wore their summer look, and suddenly I realized that it was a long while since I had spent so much time looking at hills and valleys and singing rivers.

The magazine article I read was about a man who got tired of living in big cities and went off to Vermont to run a country store. He told how it refreshed him. Before I finished reading, I almost had it in mind to run a country store myself. And I had a feeling of refreshment too. Something inside me seemed a bit starved. Maybe the Lord had me take that train journey to satisfy an unrecognized hunger for the grandeur and loveliness and peace of the natural world.

In a similar fashion, man longs for God. Very seldom does he say so to himself, but God made man and something of God is in man. God made us for Himself, and therefore there is an affinity between man and God. And there must be contact with Him, or there will be a dearth of satisfaction. One of the greatest men in Christian history uttered this immortal phrase: "Our souls are restless until at length they rest in Thee."

You are all familiar with the immortal story of Count Tolstoy, how he tried everything, seeking for satisfaction. He was wealthy, honored, feted, acclaimed. In his biography he says he ran through the calendar of sin without ridding himself of the annoying discontent that was in him. One day, walking in the country, he saw a peasant and observed the look of peace and happiness on the man's face. "This peasant has nothing," Tolstoy reminded himself, "and yet he seems filled with the joy of life." After some study, Tolstoy concluded that he was missing God, and so he sought God. One day in the forest he found Him, and delightful waves of life passed over him. At last he knew the answer to that inner hunger. He gives us this great conclusion: "To know God is to live."

I have a feeling that the trouble with so many people nowadays is that their hunger for God is not satisfied. Men have nervous breakdowns, inner conflicts, difficulties. We are told that mental problems are responsible for much of the illness of our time. Our forefathers were not afflicted in this manner. Why? Because they had a grip on God. It well may be that this generation is emotionally distraught because this hunger is not being satisfied.

I recall going one day with a friend of mine to the office of a businessman. We found this man, a publisher of a newspaper, in a very upset state of mind. He was fidgety, nervous in his reactions, strident in his conversation. Really he was under great tension. Finally he said to me, "Dr. Peale, I don't suppose you have a Bible with you?"

I didn't have one, I was sorry to admit.

"I was looking for a passage of Scripture that I wanted to use in an editorial," he explained. "I can't quite quote it. It goes something like this."

Fortunately I was able to quote the passage. Then I said, "There is another verse that might fill the bill, and possibly be even better," and I quoted it.

"You know, I sort of like that," he said.

Then the friend who was with me spoke, "I know another one that would fit in there." And he recited that.

I capped it with a further passage and watched the publisher cease to fidget. He sat back and began to talk about God. As we were leaving he said, "You know, I feel better. I am glad you came in."

On the way out my friend said, "Did you see him reach for it? We left at just the right time. You never want to oversell anybody."

That was his way of saying what I was feeling: that the man was hungry and thirsty; that he was soaking himself in God as a dirt road soaks up water after a heavy rain. He was starved, and because he was starved, he was nervous and upset. "Take my yoke upon you, and learn of me; and ye shall find rest unto your souls."

That is one of the troubles of this generation. I will venture that there are thousands of people who would have better emotional health, better physical health, a better grip on life if they would make a definite project of finding God, of getting close to Him. There is a hunger. "What means this deeper hunger in my heart?" said the poet John Oxenham. Yes, God made us for Himself. And we are never satisfied until we find Him.

How do you find Him? He is findable; He can be found. Anyone can have personal contact with God. How do you do it? The answer lies in these words: "If from thence thou shalt seek the Lord thy God, thou shalt find him, if thou seek him with all thy heart and with all thy soul." It is a fact. Anything that you really want, you can get. We all say that we want many things, but really we don't. We do not get them because that within us that knows the truth tells us we do not want them.

A fundamental law of psychology is that if—with every-thing there is in you—you reach out for something, you can get it. Emerson advised to beware of the thing that you want, for you will get it. If—down in your heart—you want some bad thing, you had better be careful or you will get it. There is another statement akin to it: "That which I have greatly feared is come upon me." If over a long period of time you fear something, you consolidate all your force; and there is danger that you will create the very thing you fear. So you had better be careful about fearing anything too much. But if with all your heart you make up your mind that you want God, that you need Him, then you will get Him. And it works sometimes in strange ways.

I once met a man who made a powerful impression on me. He asked: "Doctor, are you ever awestruck in the pulpit when you are dealing in personal conversation with God? If you are not, you ought to be. For God works in a strange and wonderful fashion."

Years ago he had become an alcoholic and was wrecking him-self physically and financially. Finally, in a hospital, he was told that there was a man in Brooklyn who seemed to have strange powers in the matter of alcoholism. This man turned out to be the founder of Alcoholics Anonymous; but he was not famous in those days.

"I went over to see him," said this man whom I will call Mr. X, "because I wanted to get well. I hoped he wouldn't talk to me about God because I had no use for God; and I didn't want to hear about this God business. If he mentioned God, I was going to walk out on him.

"I don't remember whether we talked about God at first or not," the man continued, "but I do remember Bill assured me I could overcome my trouble. 'Only you will have to put your trust in a Higher Power.

"'Do you mean God?' I asked him.

"'Yes, I mean God,' Bill said.

"'I knew you would bring up this God stuff,' I blustered. 'I am walking out. I don't want anything to do with God.'"

So Mr. X walked out the front door and down the street toward the subway. He was saying to himself, "God! God! That is all they talk about, God! I am sick of hearing about God!" And suddenly he was blinded by a white light. It seemed to be coming up from the sidewalk. The sidewalk undulated and all around him was light. It was on the faces of people whom he passed. He went into the subway, and the drab subway was suffused in light. He felt himself caught up in it. He rubbed his face with his hands asking, "What is the matter with me?"

Then he got off the train and took another back to Brooklyn and to Bill.

He told about his experience and asked, "Bill, what has happened to me?"

"Maybe you should get a New Testament and read about a man named Paul," suggested Bill. "He was down on God; he persecuted the people who were followers of God. All of a sudden there came a light out of heaven and struck Paul to the earth."

From that day, Mr. X has not been defeated. With his lips he said he did not want God. But in his soul he was crying for God. His lips said he did not want Him but his heart said, "With all my heart I truly seek Thee." Mr. X got what he really wanted, which was God.

When he told me this, it satisfied something deep within me. As I tell it to you, it satisfies something deep within you. "If from thence thou shalt seek the Lord thy God, thou shalt find him, if thou seek him with all thy heart and with all thy soul." And the deeper hungers of your nature will be satisfied. You will have a depth of peace, understanding and power you never had before.

Every human being has a story about his search for God. Many times it contains struggle, tragedy, heartache, victory, fun, delight, inspiration; you could fill a library with the glory of it. Look for this in people. Do not become so dull in your mind and in your attitude, so filled with dislikes, hates, prejudices, that you cannot see the splendor. One should learn to be very slow in his reactions to people, for when he least expects it, the glory may shine forth.

One morning in a distant city it was a quarter to ten and I had not had breakfast. I had arrived on a redeye, and after checking in at the hotel there had been some interruption every time I started to the dining room. Finally I said to myself: "I'm going to get my breakfast if I don't do another thing."

The telephone rang. A reporter was on the line. "I would like an interview," he said.

"I could give you a much better view of life after I've had some breakfast," I pleaded.

"The deadline is looming. I must see you right now. Our paper doesn't wait for breakfasts. I will be right up." He came. He bustled in, a bit cocky I thought. I tried to answer some of his questions and I began to perceive that he was a highly intelligent individual; he agreed with everything I said.

"This doctrine you are giving me is absolutely right," he said. "I am working on it myself." And he went on to tell me about the marvelous opportunity in his job of news reporting, the glorious days that lay ahead for their wonderful city.

"You interest me," I said. "I am even forgetting about my breakfast. How did you get this way?"

He reached into his pocket and pulled out a wallet and handed it to me. Inside were two pictures; one was of a beautiful girl. "My wife," he said. The other picture was of Jesus Christ. "I love them both," he said simply. "I couldn't get along without either of them. The two together give me this spirit."

As he walked to the door, he said, "It has been wonderful meeting you; I hope you get your breakfast. It is a marvelous life, isn't it?!"

For him, certainly. He had lived the passage: "If from thence thou shalt seek the Lord thy God, thou shalt find him, if thou seek him with all thy heart and with all thy soul." He had found a glorious relationship in human life and a glorious relationship in spiritual life.

This deeper hunger is not a hunger of the throat for water, nor of the eye for beauty, nor of the mind for knowledge. It is not an aesthetic hunger for nature, for hills and streams, for valleys and sunlight. It is the deeper hunger of the soul that only God can satisfy. Want Him and you will get Him. And when you get Him, you will have the answer to life. As Tolstoy said: "To know God is to live."

ON FATIGUE

Burdens and responsibilities sometimes rest so heavily that our strength seems insufficient. We become weary and tired. And it is not good to be tired unless fatigue is balanced by a normal renewal of strength. "I will strengthen the weak" (Ezekiel 34:16).

Those five plain words mean simply that when you are weak, God will strengthen you. Ever stop to consider where you get your energy? It is from God. When energy runs down and you feel weak and tired, go back to Him, and He who created your energy will recreate it. Ask God for increased energy and you will receive it. Remember the words, "In him was life." The Lord will give life energy and vitality to you if you ask it of Him and live according to His will. Thus you can overcome weakness. Tiredness will no longer be a problem.

"Let us lay aside every weight, and sin which clings so closely and us run with perseverance the race that is set before us, looking to Jesus the pioneer and perfecter of our faith" (Hebrews 12:1). One way to overcome tiredness is to lay aside the heavy weights that sap strength; such weights as fear, hate, irritation and all types of sin.

In fact, sin is the heaviest weight of all, as specifically mentioned in the above verse. And little wonder, for sin puts an abnormal burden on the mind. In time sin can become an intolerably heavy weight, so it must be laid aside if we are to run the race of life and win. Just keep Jesus in mind. He will sustain you always.

Practice faith and you need not be the victim of fatigue. Through faith you can be renewed with vitality every day. "My presence will go with you, and I will give you rest" (Exodus 33:14).

We treat ourselves very badly by driving ourselves into a state of exhaustion, straining and pushing and tugging under life's heavy weights and responsibilities. We live as though there was no unhurried flow of power available to us. Many have seemingly forgotten how to rest and renew energy. Simply become aware of God's presence, realizing that He will help you. He will show you how to work with conservation of energy, in a relaxed manner always feeling rested rather than tired. To get yourself into this manner of living frequently, say the above verses and pray on them everyday. It is generally recognized today that a direct relationship exists between spiritual and emotional attitudes and health. Many people are ill as a result of wrong thinking. Sickness and fatigue have developed so extensively in our society that a new emphasis is needed upon Christianity as a healing therapy. The previous verses are designed to help in overcoming this illness, by the Creator of all things—including energy and restfulness.

THE HAPPIEST DAY OF YOUR LIFE

He that handleth a matter wisely shall find good:
and whoso trusteth in the Lord, happy is he.

–Proverbs 16:20

What would you name as the happiest day of your life? That is an intriguing question. Many answers are suggested as we travel back along the pathway of memories. Was it one of those childhood Christmas Eves, aglitter with lights and romance and mystery? Was it perhaps the day you earned your first dollar and took it home proudly to put in the hands of your mother? Was it, let us say, the time of your first great victory or success? Or it might have been that excited time when you graduated from high school or college. Perchance it was some perfumed evening when the loveliest voice you ever heard said "yes" to your ardent proposal. Then there was the day when, awestruck, you gazed upon the face of your firstborn baby. These are all momentous, marvelous days in the lives of human beings. I suppose I could continue to list them indefinitely. But wonderful, as these days are, they do not, in my judgment, answer the question.

I should like to place as a kind of foundation under this talk a statement from the Book of Proverbs: "Whoso trusteth in the Lord, happy is he." There is little use talking about human happiness, or any so-called happiest day, unless it is reinforced with this philosophy. "Whoso trusteth in the Lord, happy is he." How can this bring about the happiest day in your life? Because when you fully trust in the Lord, when you take the Lord's presence and His ideas sufficiently into your mind so that you become a released person, the minute you do that, the very second in which it is done, you enter into the essence of the happiest experience that a human being can undergo. From that instant you begin building a superstructure of happiness.

First, the happiest day you will ever live is the day you get the glorious realization that you can defeat any weakness you have; the day you realize that you can solve any problem; the day you are conscious in your soul that you can rise victorious over any defeat. A human being on the average never does realize himself. I will venture to assert that ninety-nine percent of the people, and I am including myself, have never realized themselves. I have heard it said that most men spend their entire lives perfecting their faults. That is, you acquire a fault when you are young, emphasize it all the rest of your life, and finally die with it.

There is resident in human nature an enormous power, an immense reservoir of force. William James, father of American psychology, said that the greatest discovery of the nineteenth century was not in the realm of materialistic science; the greatest discovery was the power of the subconscious mind touched by faith. The mind is not divided into parts, but there are two levels to it. There is the conscious level where we make decisions, and the subconscious level that determines very largely what those decisions will be. It is like an iceberg, one-eighth above the water, the other seven-eighths below the surface. In every human being there is that immense reservoir of human power that, when touched by God, can overcome any difficulty in this world. I have said this before and I am going to say it again. I need constantly to be reminded of this fact myself, and therefore it is my God-given duty to remind you of it also. If you are letting anything defeat you, it is absolutely and solely because you have agreed that it should be so. That is a fact.

This power is tremendous. Let me illustrate. In the newspaper some months ago I saw an account of a woman who was in a garage where her husband was working under an automobile. The jack fell off the wheel in such a way that he was pinned down and could not extricate himself. There was no one to help the man except his wife, a woman of only average strength. Yes, there were two: there was God and there was the immense power within herself, a power that emerges under extraordinary crises. She put her hands under the car and lifted it enough so that her husband could wiggle out. When she tried to lift the car later, she could not budge it. Where did the power come from? From outside? There is no power outside. The power was inside her, and she was able to lay hold of it in this emergency.

There is another case of a man who was physically incapacitated, or, what is just as bad, he thought he was. For if you are handicapped in your mind, it is worse than being handicapped in your body. This man was wheeled down to the beach in the summertime where he was the recipient of much sympathy. Of course, this was what his subconscious wanted. He had a sixteen year-old son who one day swam out too far and, tiring, began to sink. He cried for help, but there were only a few children thereabouts. Suddenly, the father sprang from the wheelchair, threw off his clothes, dived into the sea and swam sturdily until he had brought his son to shore. He never sat in that wheelchair again. Where did he get this strength? Outside himself? No: inside, which goes to show that there is an enormous reservoir of power in every individual, if he only realizes it.

It is for this reason that Jesus says: "If ye have faith as a grain of mustard seed...nothing shall be impossible unto you." When He says that, He is pointing His finger directly at this tremendous power in the individual. When you are defeated by everything that comes along in life, you are not happy. But when the day dawns that you get a sense of this power, then you acquire a sublime confidence in yourself and you are willing to take a chance on your power.

If you are defeated by anything, the one glorious moment in your life will be when you make up your mind that nothing in this world will ever defeat you again. Because the moment you make up your mind that nothing can defeat you, that very moment nothing can defeat you.

I hesitate to use a personal illustration, but I have been so impressed by this experience that since I am sure to tell it sooner or later I might as well do it now. Yesterday I was at my alma mater, Ohio Wesleyan University in Delaware, Ohio, where I made two talks. I made one at the annual banquet of my fraternity; then I dedicated a memorial chapel to the men and women of the university who died in the wars.

I was sitting on the platform, waiting to speak. Through a huge window I could look out on the campus to the steps of Gray Chapel, which, though very old, is the principal building of the university. I remembered that on the fourth step from the bottom I had had—when I was a student—one of the greatest experiences of my life. I could see that fourth step from where I was sitting.

First, let me give you a little background. As a boy I was afflicted by shyness; I was just about the shyest individual the good Lord ever created, so much so that I hesitated to go into a room where there were strangers. I used to spend my summers with my grandmother and grandfather in a little town in southern Ohio. There was a wonderful barn out back.

In that town the minister made regular calls among the people, and it was always a great event when he came. Everybody got dressed up for the visit, which lasted a long time. However, there was a terrible custom connected with those visits, that of showing off the children by making them speak pieces for the minister. I got so that whenever the minister came I was unavoidably absent. I can remember my uncle coming around the barn where I lurked and taking me by the ear. "Norman," he said, "I am ashamed of you. You are a disgrace to the family. The minister is here and you haven't been in to speak to him." He led me by the ear, stood me in front of the minister and told me to speak my piece. I disliked that uncle for years; now I love him.

Then somehow I, who grew cold and physically sick when I had to enter a room of strangers, got the idea that I wanted to be a speaker. I had a terrible time with that thought. I hated it because every time I had to stand up before people I went through agony.

In this university, at the end of my freshman year, a professor who had great insight said to me: "Norman, you could amount to something if you had any manhood in you. But you are a weak-kneed willy-nilly. You are afraid of everything. Why don't you make a man of yourself?"

I can remember yet how mad that made me. I walked through the hall saying to myself, "I am going to leave this school. And the first thing I will do after I leave is to come back and get that professor!" What I planned to do to the man would make one of the most sadistic tales you ever heard.

I started down the steps of the chapel and I heard off in the distance somewhere the sound of religious music; it was a hymn. I got down to the fourth step from the bottom and I stopped. I said to myself: "Why don't you get over this fear business right now? Why don't you stop it?" And on that fourth step from the bottom I prayed and asked the Lord to help me stop it, and the Lord said to me: "Will you just stop being afraid?" And I said, "Yes, Lord. I'll stop being afraid."

I have always thought that the combination of prayer and being mad at that professor is what did the job. But I walked down those remaining steps and across the campus, and I can remember yet that feeling of exultation. I didn't need to be afraid anymore.

Now I didn't get over my fears just like that, but I started the process. And as I sat there yesterday, looking out through that window, remembering back over the thirty-two years since it had happened, I had a warmth in my heart, a thrill in my mind and a new birth of joy and happiness.

You don't need to be defeated by a single thing in this life if you make up your mind that you won't be; and if at the same time you put your trust absolutely in God. "Whoso trusteth in the Lord, happy is he." The happiest day in your life is when you get the inner realization of your own power touched by God and the conviction that no weakness, no problem can defeat you.

ON TROUBLES

My flesh and my heart faileth: but God is the
strength of my heart, and my portion for ever.

–Psalm 73:26

The midnight stillness was broken by the strident, insistent ringing of the telephone. A moment before its summons, after putting
away my last papers before retiring, I stood at my library window
looking out over the moonlit city. At that hour its restlessness
yields to a seeming, ineffable peace. The moonlight was tracing
a silver pathway across Central Park; and I reflected that, idylli-
cally beautiful though the world was, probably there were hearts
and minds in that moon-drenched night heavily burdened and
troubled. Then via the long-distance telephone there came a voice
calling for help.

It was the voice of an old, old friend; a strong, self-sufficient
man—at least it had always seemed so. But now he was saying: "Norman, I am tired. I was never so tired in my life. I am
exhausted. It has added up and added up and added up until I
can't take it any longer. The heart has absolutely gone out of me."

There was an interruption in the conversation, and I thought the connection had been broken until I became aware that at the other end of the wire a man whom I had never known to cry was sobbing. I gave him what emergency treatment I could over the telephone and bandaged his wounds as much as possible, pending a more definite treatment.

But after our talk was concluded, I sat reflecting upon the ways of human nature, which have been the same from time immemorial. Again and again in the literature of the world, especially in biblical literature, we read: "I am poured out like water, and all my bones are out of joint: my heart is like wax." There came to me a line from the seventy-third Psalm: "My flesh and my heart faileth: but God is the strength of my heart."

There you have the formula of human nature; the heart, the essence of us, the very center of us, fails even as the flesh fails. We become tired, weary, disheartened, without heart. But there is an answer and it is so simple. God is the strength of your heart. God restores the inner life and vitality and courage and joy. God puts heart into you.

How is it done? How do the disheartened get new heart as a result of their faith in God? First, I should say, God gives to the individual that wonderful formula known as a philosophy of difficulty. A philosophy of difficulty means that you must recognize the fact that everybody must have his share of trouble. That is the way the world is made. No matter how well you protect yourself, how well you surround yourself with security, trouble is going to get in and get at you. You can ward a lot of it off by having faith and by being sensible, using your intellect and your powers of the spiritual life. But it will touch you to a certain extent because everybody has his share.

Perhaps it is a good thing for a person to have trouble. I am not in favor of it. I have no enthusiasm for it. But fortunately I did not make the universe. If I had made it, I probably would have been foolish enough to have made everything easy. We even have certain politicians who claim they are going to fix everything so that it will be all sweetness and light, and nobody will have to worry any more because the government will take care of everyone from the cradle to the grave. Of course, that will cost a lot of money, and the government will have to take all your money away from you to pay the bills; but they do not mention that hardship.

I got into a taxicab the other day and the driver was about the maddest man I have ever seen. He had a wizened orange in his hand and shook it at me. "How much do you think that orange cost me?" he yelled. "Thirteen cents! And that isn't all. When I take this car to the garage, they take five percent of all I make away from me. It is some kind of a tax. And the government sent me a bill the other day for taxes on my tips. They don't know what the tips amount to so they guess and send me a bill for sixty-nine dollars. I thought they were going to take care of the poor! That is what they said!"

"That is what they told you," I agreed. "But they can't, they can't make life easy for you. All they are doing for you is to make it hard."

Any foolish individual who goes around telling people that things are going to be fixed so they will not have any more troubles is not telling the truth. It does not work that way. You cannot reconstruct human life.

Trouble is part of the universe; it is basic. When they first manufactured golf balls, they were smooth. Then some duffer discovered that after he got a few nicks in his golf ball he got more distance; the nicks seemed to counteract the resisting forces of the air. And so they put dimples in golf balls.

Trouble and difficulty make people; it made the American people. I never went much for Tom Paine's philosophy because he was just a poor kind of agnostic in the days of the American Revolution. He was later hopelessly outmoded and still is. But he said one thing at Valley Forge that seems to me infinitely wise: "Let us thank God for this crisis for it gives us the opportunity to prove that we are men." Adversity makes men.

A bright child was taken to a psychiatrist in this city. The child was able to develop all sorts of pain to evade any difficulty. The psychiatrist decided the child had not met enough trouble and advised the parents to manufacture adversity. "If you don't, she will grow up too soft to meet the difficulties of human existence."

This is all part of a philosophy of trouble that may comfort you a bit the next time you encounter difficulty. A continuation of the philosophy emphasizes the fact that when you get the clear-mindedness of God so that you are able to decide how to handle trouble, you just keep right at a problem until you come through to a solution. One of the great things about this world is that it does not make any difference how disheartening circumstances are, they will ultimately change. One of the most comforting facts about human existence is, "Even this shall pass away." Maybe there is no permanency to happiness; but there is no permanency to trouble either. They both pass away. If you can retain enough stick-to-it-iveness in the midst of disheartenment to keep going, you will come out on the other side of any trouble.

I remember an old friend who told me: "I got my philosophy of trouble. When I see a difficulty in front of me I go around one side of it. If I can't get around that side, I come back and go around to the other side. And if I can't get around it either way, I try to get underneath it. If I can't get underneath it, I try to get up over it. And if I can't get underneath it or above it, I just plow right smack through it. And," he said triumphantly, "like in a tunnel, you will always come out into the light. You always will if you just take up your belt and pull up your heart and keep on going."

When I was a boy I used to be in many businesses. I always did believe in free enterprise. I worked hard: I sold aluminum; I sold books; I worked in a drug store; I clerked in a department store and can remember taking down bolts of goods and putting them back. I worked in a candy store, which was a great mistake—it started me on the wrong path. I sold newspapers and had a route delivering a Cincinnati paper in a small Western Ohio town. This went very well until one afternoon my mother met me on the main street of town coming out of a bar.

"Norman," she asked sharply, "what were you doing in that place?"

"I have all the bars on my paper route."

I left the newspaper that afternoon under my mother's pressure.

Then I went into the grocery business. I worked for an old-fashioned grocer and I would not have missed that experience for the world. These newfangled stores can't compare with the old-style grocery. Just the smell of that store was wonderful. It was a mixture of pickles and coffee and cheese. The coffee was freshly ground for each customer in an old-fashioned grinder, and I never smelled such coffee. Then there was a great round cheese, and everybody who came into the store would take a big knife and whack himself off a piece and reach down into a barrel and get a handful of crackers and eat them with the cheese.

That is the kind of grocery store I worked in. And the man who owned it made money too. He used to leave me in front when there wasn't much business and go off into a back room. I found out once what he was doing back there. He knelt on an old carpet beside a box and prayed. He had a lot of troubles and he used to tell me about prayer.

One day when it was bitter cold and snowing hard and there were no customers because the streets were piled high with drifts, he came out of that prayer room and stood looking out the window at the storm. "Norman," he said, "did you ever stop to think that spring always comes? It doesn't make any difference how much winter we have, spring always comes."

Now, moods settle down and you get discouraged. Everything seems to conspire to defeat you and you complain, "Why does everything go wrong?" Sometimes deep, profound tragedy comes to you and it is very dark, very cold, and there seems to be no hope. How long have you lived? Have you ever seen a year when spring did not come? "If winter comes, can spring be far behind?"

Well, your heart and your flesh faileth, but there is strength in your heart with God. That is the way God made the world. So take up your belt, pull up your heart and keep going.

The man who knows God knows that there is a deep balance, compensation and philosophy in the universe; that if he has to say, "My flesh and my heart faileth," he will also say, "God is the strength of my heart." Because always, if you hold on and keep your feet in a sturdy place and keep your heart substantial, you will come through.

That is one way to get new heart when you are disheartened. The other is a very simple one; it is so simple that you will think when I suggest it that I haven't told you anything. But I have lived long enough to be absolutely sure of this. You can pray your way through any difficulty the world or the devil ever conspired to put in front of you. Prayer is the greatest technique God ever gave us. If you will pray and keep on praying and pray some more, there isn't any difficulty that need dishearten you. You will get your heart back by prayer.

If you are in a difficulty right now, if you are discouraged, disheartened about anything, quit talking about it; quit fuming and fretting about it; quit complaining about it; quit going around and trying to get advice about it. Start praying about it and yield yourself to God in prayer. Ask Him for the answer; ask Him for His answer, not yours. And stay with Him. The Bible has words about "Being in an agony he prayed more earnestly," about "The kingdom of heaven suffereth violence and the violent take it by force," about "Prayer was made without ceasing." Why does it tell you to pray without ceasing? Because if you pray without ceasing, you get your whole mind and your life conditioned so that God can do great things for you as a result of your prayers. He wants to help you before you have ever said a word of prayer. But He has to get you conditioned before the great things can be done. Just pray, that is all. It is very simple. If you are disheartened about anything, just pray and keep on praying.

I have a friend who is forty-one years old and totally blind. He was chairman of a meeting at which I spoke in Savannah, Georgia.

He had made all the arrangements for the meeting, and it was one of the best organized that I ever addressed. Everybody in that town loves him. When we checked in at the hotel, we were taken to the eighth floor. As we left the elevator, he said, "Turn to the left."

"How do you know that?" I asked.

"Because I have my wits about me," he said. "I come to this hotel often. All the even numbers are on the left, the odd numbers on the right."

I watched him walking down the hall. "I have forgotten the number of my room," I said. "Do you remember it?"

"It is the next door," he said.

All day long it was like that. He knew details I didn't know. We were going to the television station for an interview on the air and inquired about directions. We both listened. But on the street I would have walked by the building if he had not stopped me. "Where are you going?" he said. "Here it is. Right here." "How do you do it?" I asked.

"The Lord took away my sight, but He gave me an attention to detail."

I remember when, in New York, the specialist he had come North to see gave him the terrible news that he was going blind. The doctor promised him no more than a few months. He went back to the hotel where he was staying, went to his room, walked over and looked out of the window. It was a clear day in Manhattan and the sun was shining. He looked down on the people walking along the street. "Some of them look very poor," he said to himself, "but they can see. They haven't just been told that they are going blind. I would give everything I have ever had or hope to have; I would be willing to be as poor as the poorest if I could only see for the rest of my life." And he added, "Why do I want to live if I am going to be a blind man?" He looked at the window. "It would only take a minute. There would be the effort of it; then there would be one wild moment of terror; and then it would be over and I would be at peace."

He told me how he had gripped that window sill; how, resisting the thought, he went down on his knees instead of going out of the window. He prayed almost continuously for twenty-four hours. He had never prayed like that before in his life. He said, "I got into it and I just agonized with God. Then, all of a sudden, I had a burst of light. It wasn't in my eyes; it was in my brain. I knew God was telling me, 'Son, I can't give you back your eyesight, but I will give you power greater than you have ever had.' And He has."

The Bible says: "My flesh and my heart faileth." But it also says, "God is the strength of my heart." So just take your trouble, whatever it is, and start praying about it until light comes in your brain and you feel a good old sturdiness in your heart once again. And you will have new heart for all the disheartenment that you will ever face.

A COURSE THROUGH THE STORM

Not that I speak in respect of want: for I have learned,
in whatsoever state I am, therewith to be content.

–Philippians 4:11

One of the most amazing inspirations in this world is the manner in which people meet and overcome the difficulties of human existence. In the nature of my work and activity, it has been my privilege to have close contacts with human beings, entering into their deepest experiences, their pain, suffering and sorrow. Again and again I have been astonished by the knowledge of what human nature can take. If it ever occurs to you in moments of depression to become cynical or discouraged about your fellowmen, I suggest that you consider the heroism and courage with which they meet pain, trouble, heartache and all complicated vicissitudes of human existence. The more I see of people, the more wonderful I think they are.

No tale of fiction can equal the stories written in the lives of simple, everyday men and women. People are magnificent. And the longer I deal with them, the more convinced I am that that appraisal is an accurate one. Storms of the utmost severity strike down upon their lives, sometimes out of the blue with no forewarning, and leave devastation in their wake; breaking down or brushing away the hopes and ambitions of years. But they stand up under it all. One is reminded of great old trees that have been sending down their roots into the soil among the rocks for generations. When storms strike, these are shaken; but when the storms pass, there they still stand as sturdy as ever.

Therefore, I want to raise the question: what is a safe course through the storms of life? This is not an academic question. It is one of the utmost practicality. It is well to have a formula for meeting storms and to be ready to apply it when these storms come.

One of the most interesting stories ever written, one filled with drama, and picturesque in quality, is told in a dozen lines, more or less. It is one of the most gripping stories in the literature of the world. It is about our Lord who, with His disciples, was in a small boat on the lake. These disciples were fishermen, suntanned, vigorous, who knew the ways of wind and water. But the storm that burst upon them was great, even for their experience. The sky was overcast, the lightning flashed, the winds blew and the water of the lake was whipped up into a seething mass of foam. The waves toyed with that boat sickeningly, seeking to smash it to pieces. So great was the tumult and tempest and cataclysm of sound that these experienced sailors were terrified. But they remembered their strangely gifted passenger aboard and they sought Him.

Where did they find Him? Asleep in the stern of the boat, head resting on His arm, a perfect demonstration of poise and relaxation. I have often thought how wonderful it must have been to gaze upon the face of Jesus as he slept there. So pure was His mind, so undefiled His soul, so deeply peaceful His conscious and His subconscious nature that He must have rested like a baby in the cradle of the deep. But these men cried, "Master, carest thou not that we perish?"

He opened His eyes with deliberation, He looked up at them and a slow smile crossed His face. He loved these men; He knew their quality. They were His friends. "Why are you afraid? Haven't you any faith?" Then He arose, stretched with the delicious health of body and soul that He possessed, walked across the deck, awash with water, until He had one arm around the mast. The froth from the waves drenched Him to the skin, His gown adhered to His lithe figure; His face was wet with the spray and His hair tossed by the wind. There He stood, a mighty figure, with cowering frightened human beings about Him. He raised His hand, and His voice was as clear as a silver bell ringing out over the waters. "Peace, be still." And the Bible, with its deft ability to paint pictures in a few words, says—one of the immortal passages of all time —"And there was a great calm."

I have no doubt that Jesus quieted the actual waves. But I have always wondered where this great calm was—on the water, or in the hearts of the men who looked at the water? The waves might still have been tumultuous; but the disciples were no longer afraid, for they had peace in their hearts and they knew they could steer a safe course through the storm.

What did Jesus give them, and what does He give us that will help us ride out the storms of contemporary human life? He gave them one great truth, which is that in each of us are enormous resources of power to meet difficulty. This is something everybody ought to learn about himself.

Lowell Thomas told me once about the fabled Lawrence of Arabia whom he knew very well. He said that one of the great things Lawrence often mentioned was his discovery of the fact that a human being can take incredibly more than he has ever had to take; that in tragedy a person discovers resources of power he did not know he possessed.

In other words, you are equal to any circumstance that will ever come to you. Almighty God will never allow any thing to happen to you that you cannot handle, that you cannot stand if you have faith in Him.

Captain Eddie Rickenbacker, for example, who I think is one of the most romantic figures America has ever produced, stated to me that he flirted with death a half dozen times and escaped its clutches. One time was when he crashed in an airplane years ago. They took him to the hospital, thinking he was going to die. And when he did not die they told him he would never use his right hand again. This would have been a blow to any man. Eddie lay in bed and looked at his hand. He has always been a person of simple, childlike faith. He told me he held this hand up to another doctor saying, "I believe You can heal that hand." And the doctor seemed to say to him, "You and I together will heal your hand."

Eddie asked the nurse to anchor a glass on the table. Day after day, week after week, he went to work with his fingers; calling upon God, summoning the deep inner resources of his nature; exercising faith, manhood, character—struggling to get his fingers around the glass. One day he achieved this, and today his fingers work as well as anybody's. How did he do it? He drove down deep into his nature, where there are reservoirs of power, and brought them up by manhood and faith.

You say, "He is a strong man." True. But let me tell you about a strong woman in whose home I stayed recently. She and her husband live down South, and they are great friends of mine. She is a little thing, very delicate. I like to visit her for she serves those marvelous Southern breakfasts: ham, gravy, grits, biscuits. She was told one day that she was going blind.

"Norman," she said to me, "have you any idea how a person feels when told she will never see the light of day again; never see the dew on the grass in the morning, or the long rays of the sun in the afternoon, or the light of the moon at night?"

I have often wondered about that myself—how terrible it would be—and yet people do survive it.

She told me she was petrified with fear. "I was filled with panic," she said. "I wanted to die. Then one day while doing my housework I dusted the table on which was a Bible. I opened it at random. There I read about a man who was having a lot of trouble. He said, 'I have learned, in whatsoever state I am, therewith to be content.' Of course I had read that passage many times; but all of a sudden it seemed that the great hand of Jesus came down and set me free, taking away all my fear, all my panic. I felt something welling up within me, and I never felt so strong in my life. I knew that if darkness had to come to me, I could take it."

I am glad to say that this woman received a healing faith along with that message, and under the skill of her physician her sight was saved. But I shall never forget the look on her face when she said, "I discovered that I had a power within me I never knew before that

I had. I had read your articles in which you talked about this inner power," she added, "but I had never felt it until that day."

You know how some automobiles have added power, or overdrive, or some sort of built in "turbo boost"? I have it in my car. When you press down on the accelerator, you get added speed. You drive this pedal down to the floor and gain speed quickly to pass a car on the highway. I assure you I only use it occasionally, but it is a glorious feeling. Everybody should get such a feeling within himself. But you have to press down; you really have to drive into this spiritual power. Don't let anything defeat you in this world. You do not need to because you have the power within you.

Do you know where some of the worst storms of life are? They are not the storms of adversity, of poverty, of sickness, of death, of pain. They are the storms people create in their own minds. They are the tempests in the brain and in the emotions. There is nothing so pathetic as a tempest in the brain. That is why we have so many psychiatrists and psychologists, so many mental health doctors today. Because most of the storms from which people suffer are storms in the mind.

How do these storms arise? They come from various sources. One such source is guilt, another is fear, another is hate. You begin to hate and then you let loose the winds of poisoning; or you enter into a situation that creates a fear that becomes a tornado. You do a guilty thing, you commit a sin and do not get it forgiven, or you do not forgive yourself; it lies embedded in the essence of your nature and after a while it creates tumult. These are the pathetic storms of man's own making, and it is curious how they work.

The other day I was out in the Midwest in a bookstore autographing books. I was to make a speech in the town that evening.

The manager of the store was a very good businesswoman, and because of her effective advertising I found a long line of people waiting with books to be signed. I enjoyed meeting them and was having a good time when I noticed one man: a fine-looking, well-dressed person, obviously ill at ease, who seemed very much pressed for time. Finally, he approached two or three people who were ahead of him and said that he was in a great hurry and would they mind letting him come next. To me he said, "I made a sacrifice to get here to see you today. I only came because I thought I had to." Every action was tense; he even made me tense the way he expressed himself. "I want to buy this new book of yours. I must have some help." Then he added, "I have your book *A Guide to Confident Living*, and it did me a lot of good."

To me there was no pointed evidence that it had done him much good.

"My wife gave it to me a few years ago," he explained, "because I was not sleeping nights. I found that it helped me to sleep. But I have read it so much it has lost its effect on me. It doesn't put me to sleep any more." This is actually what he said, word for word. And he meant it. He had no idea how it sounded. "So I thought maybe if I got this new book, I might get a few nights' sleep."

I said to him, "I hope this book puts you to sleep also; at least you will be getting what you paid for."

"I seem inwardly upset all the time," the man said as he left me.

Later there was a reception and this man appeared. He came to me and said, "Doctor, I have been reading something ridiculous. I get so tired of the foolish statements made by modern psychiatrists. One of them actually wrote an article claiming that the reason some people are tense and their heart action is fast and their blood pressure high is because they have an unresolved sense of guilt. Now," he went on, "you know as well as I that every young man has to commit a number of sins and that most of them do. This psychiatrist said that if those sins were not resolved, they would act as a kind of poison in the system." Then he added, "Surely that cannot be true."

"Do you want the truth or do you want me to agree with you?" I asked.

"I want the truth," he replied.

So I explained: "We know today, from the mind/body point of view, according to some doctors, that many maladies of the body are caused by diseased thoughts in the mind. Anybody who has buried in his consciousness a sense of guilt will, in all likelihood, be a victim of tension because the mind, being honest, believes that he must be punished, and so proceeds to punish him by anxiety and tension. The mind says to the individual, 'Work hard so that I, the mind, can tell you that the reason you are tense is because you are overworking.' And this binds you to the fact that you are running away from a deep, unconscious sense that you should be punished."

You should have seen the look on his face. He said, "Maybe that is it."

I had to leave him then, but I like that fellow. He is every inch a man. He has been bad, there is no question about it. But he is honest and real, and he is in great need. He will be healed of his trouble by healing his moral nature from which his trouble comes. And the cure will come when he turns to the only one who can tell the storms in his mind to subside. Jesus Christ will speak the word of peace. To quote the great old words again, "And there was a great calm."

A NOTE FROM THE EDITORS

We hope you enjoy *Navigate* by Norman Vincent Peale, published by Guideposts Books and Inspirational Media. In all of our books, magazines and outreach efforts, we aim to deliver inspiration and encouragement, help you grow in your faith and celebrate God's love in all aspects of your daily life.

We are a nonprofit organization, and your purchase of *Navigate* helps fund our many outreach programs to the military, prisons, hospitals, nursing homes and schools. We also maintain many useful and uplifting online resources for everyone in need of renewal, prayer and spiritual support.

Thank you for making a difference with your purchase. We invite you to learn more about our organization and discover how Guideposts ministries may be of service to you by visiting the following Web sites: GuidepostsFoundation.org to access an uplifting prayer network called Our Prayer and learn more about our outreach ministry; DailyGuideposts.org to sign up for daily devotional e-mails and free newsletters, download exclusive free e-books and be a part of our Facebook community; Guideposts .org to read true stories of hope and inspiration and find out about our other publications; and AngelsonEarth.org to enjoy articles about heavenly and earthly angels who have played wondrous roles in daily life.

To order your favorite Guideposts publications, go to ShopGuideposts.org, call (800) 932-2145, or write to Guideposts, PO Box 5815, Harlan, Iowa 51593.